Cyber Security For Normal People Protect Yourself Online

SADANAND PUJARI

Published by SADANAND PUJARI, 2023.

Table of Contents

Copyright

Cyber Security For Normal People Protect Yourself Online

Copyright©**SADANAND PUJARI**, 2023

Cover design by **SADANAND PUJARI**

First published in 2023 by

SADANAND PUJARI

About

A beginner level comprehensive Book that includes step-by-step explanations of core security concepts along with follow-up quizzes and hands-on labs to ensure a solid learning for the Book taker.

Designed by a CyberSecurity expert this Book has been designed to make it extremely simple to learn complex Cyber Security concepts. Designed for beginner Cyber Security professionals, this Book will help you master the major domains and launch a successful career in the Cyber Security industry. It is also a good starting point for students targeting Cyber Security certifications like CompTIA Security+ and CEH.

Introduction

Hello and welcome to Complete Introduction to Cybersecurity. By the time you complete this Book, you will have a foundational understanding of what cybersecurity is, how it's implemented, the specifics of cybersecurity, including the tools and technologies used throughout the industry, what types of threats and attacks are posed to us and companies both large and small and much more. I'll be covering all of the Book goals and objectives in the next chapter, so I'm very glad to have you join us as a prospective student enthusiast or professional.

All skill levels are welcome. So a little bit about me. I am a cybersecurity engineer, formerly a cybersecurity student. Not too long ago I ran a small YouTube channel which talks about my journey getting into cybersecurity and just general cybersecurity concepts. And I also run a small website and discord server. It's called Cyber Academy.

Now, for those of you who are just getting started, the world industry of cybersecurity can be daunting and overwhelming. You have thousands of online resources to choose from and many questions. And it may seem like, you know, getting into cybersecurity is quite impossible to break through. As a security student myself, I know exactly what type of questions you are encountering, the doubts you have in the experiences you've gone through. I'm in the exact same place myself, but through dedicated time in research, I was able to find a clear path and direction by learning the foundations of I.T. and cybersecurity and really doing these same exact things throughout this Book.

So this Book is going to give you a clear direction of what the fundamentals are in I.T. And the security components or layers that are on top of the basics. So for a general overview of this Book, we will be working through six total chapters, each one working off of each other. I will be starting with the basics of cybersecurity, covering what it is and what is involved. Out of this. I'll be transitioning into general I.T terms and terminologies and concepts to get us quickly up and running with it.

After our first couple of chapters, we'll finally move into chapters four through six where I will be covering the different types of cybersecurity attacks, defenses and how to create our very own practice lab to cover some of these concepts for practical application to get the most out of each chapter and really to get the most out of this mini Book.

I challenge you to take notes and think critically throughout the Book. Also perform additional research into the topics covered throughout this Book. This Book is going to give a great introduction to a lot of concepts, so make sure to download all worksheets and take each chapter quiz to test yourself. All right. Once again, thank you so much for joining me along this Book. I really hope that you learn a lot and are welcome.

Objectives

Let's go ahead and get started with this Book by first talking about the Book objectives and goals. So what are you going to learn and what will be accomplished throughout this Book? So throughout this Book, we're going to understand the basics of it and information security. And this is going to include the different types of domains. And we'll go over what that is, general concepts of it, attacks and defenses presented to us.

We're wanting to gain a foundational understanding of what cybersecurity is, including what it's about and how it's implemented, both on a personal level, but also in a small and large enterprise or business environment. We're going to want to develop a learning plan for next steps, and this includes anywhere from general to cybersecurity. Student If you're looking to launch into your own learning journey and we're going to want to be able to apply any abstract concept into practical learning. This is a key component in our learning process.

Taking an abstract concept, you know, a concept we briefly go over and actually implementing this with a certain tool, technology or thought process, and then we're going to want to develop a working small scale project or practice environment to learn and simulate some cybersecurity concepts. And this is going to include the use of tools, technologies and much more. And this is going to be our last chapter where we're going to be setting up both virtual and cloud environments where we can practice some of what we've learned in this Book. So these are the objectives in the scope we will be covering throughout this Book. Each objective is really going to contribute towards the overall goal of getting you started in it in a more specific way.

Effective Note Taking

Effective note taking is an imperative process which will really enhance your ability to conceptualize and learn throughout the classroom. Of course, for this Book, I highly recommend that you get out a notepad or you go onto Microsoft Word or Google Docs and write down notes. As you progress through this Book, I want to briefly show you how I take effective notes when it comes to Books that I am completing.

Now, Of course, there's two ways you can take notes. One is through the standard notepad and pen and pencil. This is going to be a good way for you to go ahead and conceptualize the knowledge and a better way because you are writing it down now. It is a little slower and I tend to use a Google Docs or word document to take notes. Let's go ahead and transition over to my computer where I'm going to display how I take effective notes throughout Books here in front of me. I have an introduction to Active Directory Book notes. Don't worry about the content.

I'm more specifically focused on how I go about writing my notes. So here in front of me, what I like to do is go ahead and include the chapter resource, perhaps the chapter title throughout my Book that you can add. And then I like to go ahead and work through the different types of components or points that are mentioned throughout the PowerPoint or throughout the presentation. And what I like to do is look up different types of examples or I like to look up different types of keywords if they are not expanded upon within the Book. As you can see, what I like to do is go ahead and title each chapter in bold with the specific chapter, and here I go ahead and jot down the points that are made within the PowerPoints.

Now the PowerPoints or presentations are included within the download chapter of the files. You can go ahead and download those in PDF format to have a complete set of notes and then you can go ahead and expand upon them through notepad and paper pencil, or you can do a Google Docs very simple process It's really going to help you conceptualize the knowledge and truly internalize what you're learning throughout this Book. So let's go ahead and get started with chapter two.

[Hands-on Attack Scenario] Download Virtual Machine

In the preceding chapters, there will be a hands-on cyber attack scenario denoted by the [Hands-on Attack Scenario] prefix. You can refer to chapter 9 in chapter 2 of this Book to understand an overview of the attack. This will be a simple, basic attack. I encourage you to follow along. Download the file below (Icedrive Link). This download will allow us to set up the attack in a contained, isolated environment. You can proceed to the next chapter if you do not wish to download the file at this time.

Virtual Machine (VM) Image:

https://ln5.sync.com/dl/f63d70fa0/u2qxmdbp-estw35d6-txungxp8-ineutwps

Make sure to take note of where you downloaded this file. It will be named "Attack Scenario 1.ova."

For Windows machines, the default download directory is:

C:\Users\YourUserName\Downloads

For Mac macOS machines, the default download directory is:

/Users/YourUserName/Downloads/

NOTE: This file will take several hours to download (it's 17.15 Gigabytes), depending on Internet connection. Make sure to start the download process now to follow along with the preceding chapters prefixed with [Hands-on Attack Scenario].

NOTE: The [Hands-on Attack Scenario] and VirtualBox will not work with Apple macOS m1 or m2 processors.

What is Cybersecurity?

In this chapter, we are going to cover what cybersecurity is, where and how it's implemented, and further break down the word cybersecurity into the different domains that cybersecurity is often categorized in. All right. So let's go ahead and start off with chapter two by defining what cybersecurity is. So cybersecurity is the combination of people, processes and technology that come together to protect organizations, computer systems, networks and individuals from the theft or damage of hardware, software or any type of data from disruption, misdirection or corruption. So that's a very wordy definition here.

Let's go ahead and break this down and extract the core components from this definition. So cybersecurity ultimately comes down to risks. How will cyber risks pose to an organization, impact business processes and the organization as a whole? Now, a risk can be posed to an organization really can be indirect or direct. So a direct example could be a targeted attack on a network of computers. As an indirect example, an unplanned weather storm could destroy a network or data center full of computers and servers.

Even though both of these scenarios are under very different circumstances, they both present potential risks to disrupt business processes. So cybersecurity risk is the probability of exposure or loss resulting from a cyber attack or data breach. And this can be extended to a large scale business or average home users such as you and I, depending on the type of motive and scale cybercriminals perform attacks to take advantage of really an open area on the internet.

At the end here, this statement talks about misdirection, corruption and disruption of hardware, software or data. Now misdirection, corruption and disruption can be replaced here with confidentiality, integrity and availability. Confidentiality, integrity and availability are the core of cybersecurity. Each one of these components impacts the overall risk posed to an organization. Confidentiality, integrity and availability are commonly referred to as the CIA Triangle or CIA Triad.

If you study any type of introductory cybersecurity certification or introductory class, you will most likely see this term defined at the very beginning of the class. So as I stated here, the CIA triangle is the core to cybersecurity. In addition to the CIA triad, there are other components to cybersecurity, which are also considered like authentication, authorization, accounting and non-repudiation. There's a common model known as the CI, a N, where you have authentication and non-repudiation ensuring that hardware, software and data is kept confidential means that only the intended individuals' slash systems are able to view that information.

Being able to maintain integrity means that values have not been altered or changed from the original sender receiver. Ensuring the system and data is able to be viewed and accessed when queried to do so. Really, this is the core to cybersecurity and it comes down to these three components in addition to the other ones I've talked about. So now that we've loosely defined what cybersecurity is, it's time to define where cybersecurity or how cybersecurity is implemented.

Where is Cybersecurity Implemented?

Cybersecurity can take form in many ways, depending on how you interpret, define and apply the word cybersecurity. Given the context is really important, cybersecurity can take the form of being a process, a strategy, a service, a product or technology, a skill, a program and much more.

Let's go ahead and quickly define what each of these is. So cybersecurity can be a process where you have implemented management systems, governance frameworks, best practices, policies and procedures to reduce risk. And we'll go over what each of these means in the next chapter. Cybersecurity can be a strategy. So this is where specific policies, procedures, systems, services and personnel are allocated to mitigate a set of risks. Cybersecurity can be a service such as a company providing a set of services.

This could be a security consulting company, an auditing type process, which is the process of reviewing how certain processes are managed or executed and designing, hardening and recovery. Really, any of these can be services. Cybersecurity can be a product such as an antivirus program, a firewall or a system to help you manage security alerts. It can be a skill such as being able to develop a computer network from a security standpoint. This could be dealing with and mitigating security alerts.

Identifying or hardening a system could be pen testing, managing a team of security professionals, being an auditor, really, cybersecurity has a lot of different types of skills and it's very broad. And cybersecurity can be an entire program where you have specific tasks: security controls, personnel products and services working to detect, protect, mitigate and recover from all of or any of the risks posed to an organization. So this is cybersecurity as a program, working in an organization as a whole. But then you also have other types of programs like software programs. So there are a lot of different implementations cybersecurity can be manifested into.

The Six Cybersecurity Domains

When starting out with the cybersecurity industry, you will probably stumble upon a lot of media and marketing and Hollywood depictions of cybersecurity, and this is most likely someone who is in a dark room with green lines of code, wearing a dark hoodie or some sort of picture like that. Now, as a very beginner in cybersecurity, this may stand out as a particular media depiction, but the word cybersecurity encompasses really an entire field of professions, services and responsibilities, something that we briefly overviewed in the last chapter, especially applied to the context of business in cybersecurity.

Really, it has an expansive outreach of different types of responsibilities. So what is a cybersecurity domain? Really, a cybersecurity domain relates back to the overall definition, goal and mission of cybersecurity, and this is to reduce a set of risks posed to a business and how this will impact business operations. Now, depending on who you ask and where you learn from, there will be a set of domains listed as the official set of domains of cybersecurity. For the sake of this Book, I have categorized the domains of cybersecurity into six domains: security, architecture, risk assessment, threat, intelligence, governance, risk and compliance known as GRC, security operations and physical security.

Listed number of domains may vary in title or chapter under the different definitions. The order and specific title really don't matter in this particular case as long as we cover the main ones like a Book like this one. So let's go ahead and overview each one starting with security architecture. So security architecture is the unified security design, which focuses on setting security principles, methods and models designed to align with business and security objectives.

Security architecture consists of preventative detective and corrective security controls that are implemented in an enterprise infrastructure for applications. Now, there will be a difference between how security architecture is implemented depending on the size and scale of a business. Security architecture considers building a secure system by design from the ground up and then actively maintaining the system with really an active approach and system could mean an application such as software program or network, or it can mean something entirely different. So it means a lot of different things.

Domain is a risk assessment. Risk assessment is a combined effort used to describe the overall process or method of identifying and analyzing potential hazards which could negatively impact your business processes, environments, individuals, assets and more. Now, in the context of information security, risk assessment is used to identify, estimate and prioritize risks posed to the operations of information systems and IT. Infrastructure Risk assessment is a business concept and considers the monetary gains and losses of a Business. An organization will need to consider how money is made, how employees and assets affect the profitability of business, and what risks More particularly, cyber risks could result in large monetary losses to a business. Next domain is threat intelligence.

Threat Intelligence is the evaluation and collection of information about cyber threats and threat actors. This information can be used to prevent losses to an organization and mitigate harmful events from happening now. Threat Intelligence is the collection of various sources of information, and this can include open source intelligence such as social media, human, technical, deep or dark web, and much more. Threat intelligence is about providing context into who is attacking your organization or an organization, what are their motivations and their capabilities, and how you can identify when you have been compromised by one of these threats.

Next is governance, risk and compliance, or often abbreviated as GRC. GRC are three facets aimed to ensure that a business meets objectives while maintaining integrity in

continuing business processes. Now governance is the combination of processes executed by business directors to lead an organization toward building goals and maintaining organizational structure. We've briefly already overviewed risks, but risk management is about predicting and managing risks which could impact the organization from reliably achieving objectives and goals. And then finally, compliance.

This is about establishing and allowing mandatory laws and regulation in addition to following voluntary company policies, procedures, guidelines and standards. So together, governance, risk and compliance is used to reliably achieve business objectives under periods of uncertainty while maintaining integrity. Next is security operations. Now, security operations involve the day to day security activities. Security Operations is a centralized unit which deals with organizational and technical security. Issues. Security operations often take the form of what is known as a security operations center or SOC.

A SOC is a centralized location or facility where staff and monitoring systems reside in a security operations center. An organization is concerned with protecting the daily functions of business, network and services running in the business. So a SOC is in charge of really protecting, preventing and then finally detecting, containing, recovering and then investigating network events happening on a daily basis or security events. Now these events could be a network attack on a specific area of a company. And then finally, we have physical security. Now, physical security is concerned with protecting and dealing with physical threats and events from happening.

This includes the protection of personnel, controlling who and where access is granted to hardware, software, networks and data. Now, physical security also considers protection from natural disasters such as fire, flood and then other types of natural disasters. School security is often an overlooked component of cyber security. So these six domains make up what we know as cyber security. Each of these domains have a specific set of goals and responsibilities to actively manage cyber security risk. All right.

So now that we know what cyber security is, how it's implemented and some general domains of cybersecurity, it's finally time to get into our first technical kind of hands on chapter here. We will be reviewing some common IT terminologies and some concepts involved with basic IT. So we'll see you in chapter three. This is really where it ramps up here to get into it. And cybersecurity.

[Hands-on Attack Scenario]
Introduction

Throughout the duration of this Book, we're going to be walking through a mock scenario which will demonstrate how an effective security attack can take place in a business environment. We will be setting up a computer machine known as a virtual machine, which is going to act as our victim. Now, due to the limitations of this scenario, there will be software and tooling already installed on the victim machine.

And I'm going to highlight when there is preloaded software and how it actually be installed in a real life situation from the attacker's point of view. So what's the basis of this attack? Well, an attacker wants to gain initial access to a victim machine, and in this case, the attacker has chosen a finance worker for a small to medium sized business.

The finance employees machine is a virtual machine which will be downloaded here momentarily. The attacker has been able to gain insightful information about this business from the business website, specifically in the About Us page, which lists the executive boards with their full names and a short description of their career backgrounds. The attacker has launched an email spreading campaign where they've gathered some potential leads, which in this case is email addresses from an underground dark web form.

Now, using this information, the attacker has crafted an email to be sent to all email addresses ending with the at dot.com address. The attacker is wanting to target the accounting department in this case, and since they don't know who specifically works in the accounting department, they will be crafting an email message which is generic to the address, but specific to all employees of the business. Make sure to follow along within our mock scenario while following the core chapters of this Book.

In this case, the chapter chapters with the prefix attack scenario indicate the content pertaining to this scenario. Before we proceed forward, let's go ahead and download a file ova file, which is a virtual machine, and it will allow us to set up the attacker scenario later in this Book. So in the description below or up on the screen here, I'll be pasting in a sync.com link which contains the OVA file. Now this file is very big.

It's 17.1GB and this will probably take several hours to download depending on your internet connection. So all you can do is just click download and then make sure to keep track of where this is downloaded. Typically it's going to be in your downloads folder. Later in this Book, we're going to go ahead and actually set up this attacker machine.

Types Of Network

In this chapter, I will be lecturing over the different types of hardware, software and network components involved in basic IT. So let's go ahead and go over what we'll be overviewing specifically in chapter three. Starting off, we will be covering the basics of computing, starting with the physical components of computer hardware.

I'll be covering common computing devices and those internal components that make up the computing devices and we will be covering the different types of storage to store computer data and files. From there, I'll be reviewing software, including the different types of operating systems and the purpose of software. Then transitioning into the network side.

Inside the network chapter, we will be reviewing common terms and models used for what makes up the internet today. And finally, I will be briefly reviewing the cloud, including what it is and the different types of models involved. So we have a lot to cover in the IT Fundamentals chapter. Let's go ahead and get started with hardware.

Computer Hardware

Computing devices are everywhere. Devices like computers, tablets and mobile phones are used around us every day. So what is a computing device? Well, a computing device is any electronic device or machine used to perform calculations automatically. Now, that is a very broad statement there. And we'll digest this down a little bit as we continue to define the different types of components involved in computing devices.

Now, computing devices function through the basic process of input and output. Input is to provide or give something to the computing device where the computing device waits to receive a command or signal. Upon receiving some type of input, the computing device interprets and processes this input into some output and this is where output is generated. We are participating in the process of input and output every time we use a computing device really without even knowing it. So there are all types of input and output devices, examples of input devices could be including typing

keys into our keyboard, moving the mouse around our screen or taking a photo using a digital camera.

Also, we could be talking into a microphone or using a joystick from a gaming controller. Now, upon receiving this input from the input device, output is generated. This output can be interpreted as something meaningful to the user. Now, examples of output devices include computer monitors, a printer, headphones, speakers and projectors. The process of input and output is how information is created, generated, and how computing devices are used to interpret and process this information into meaningful output for US users.

As a result, from this process, we can actually use our input to store our information for future uses. The process of input and output is measured in units. Units are used to measure the capacities of systems and data channels in computing. When information is supplied to a computer through the process of input, this information is broken down into binary. Binary consists of either a 0 or 1. A zero means off and a one means on in terms of electronic signals.

Now we call a single 0 or 1 a bit, and it's really a single unit of information. It has a value of either on or off. If we put eight bits together, they form a byte. Now, if we put 1000 bytes together, these form a kilobyte and so on and so on. So what this means is that units create measurements for how we store information and how it's created, generated and really stored. We interact with computing devices every day. As I've stated, common computing devices include laptops, mobile devices, tablets, computer workstations, servers, gaming consoles and Internet of Things devices. And this can include appliances, home automation, cameras and medical devices.

We can also use external or peripheral devices which operate separately but are connected to common computing devices. These include printers, scanners, keyboards, mouses, cameras, external hard drives, speakers, displays and gaming controllers. So now that we have an overview of computing components, let's go ahead and overview the internal computing components which make up a common computing device.

Internal Computing Components

Now that we know what a computing device is, the process of input and output and how we measure data, let's go ahead and take a look at the internal components of computing devices and how they work to accomplish what we now know as a common computing device. Let's take a computer workstation, which is commonly known as a PC tower or desktop, and this is going to be the example we use to look inside the internal components of the PC. So when we open up the PC, we will see multiple internal components connected together depending on the make and model of your PC.

The first component which will probably stand out is the motherboard. The motherboard is a printed circuit board used as the foundation of a computer. The motherboard allocates power and it allows communication between other internal computing components such as the CPU Ram and other hardware components. There are multiple types of motherboards designed to work with a specific type of processor and memory. So the motherboard will connect a lot of components together. And one of these is the CPU.

Now the CPU stands for Central processing Unit, the CPU handles and executes instructions it receives from hardware and software running on the computer. A CPU performs basic arithmetic logic and input output operations specified by instructions within the program. A CPU is often referred to as the brain of the computer. It's what allows you to process information. Ram is a form of computer memory that can be read and changed in any order. Ram is often used to store and work with data in machine code and allows information to be stored and retrieved on a computer in almost the same amount of time. Whereas any other direct access data storage devices such as hard drives are much slower. Mem is used by the CPU.

When the computer needs to store information, it needs to be used very quickly but does not need to be stored permanently because the information is accessed randomly instead of in a sequential order. Ram is very fast. Ram also requires power to keep data accessible, so if the computer is turned off, all data contained within Ram is lost. Now, in addition to the CPU and Ram, the motherboard also connects other types of internal components as well. And this can include the GPU storage devices. And Nic, GPU stands for graphic processing unit.

Graphic processing units are used to speed up the creation of 2D and 3D images. A GPU can be integrated, meaning it's already built within the CPU or motherboard, or it can be dedicated, meaning it's a separate piece of hardware. So if you are in the gaming community, you will often find that a lot of gamers want to have a dedicated GPU for better graphics processing. There are multiple different types of storage devices used when storing information in computing devices. Some of the common devices include hard drives and solid state drives or SSDs. Now SSDs and hard drives are non-volatile data storage devices. So that means when the power is turned off, the data is kept.

Now SSDs are considered faster than hard drives because really they have no moving parts and a hard drive. There is a disk whereas an SSD there is no disk. In addition to storage devices, we also have NICs or network interface cards. So these are also referred to as Ethernet or network adapters. Nic is a computer expansion card used to connect to a network. So right now think of a Nic as a means to connect you to the Internet to provide power to all components inside a computer. Power supplies are utilized, power supplies convert AC or alternating current into steady low voltage DC direct current, which is usable by the computer. So this is how the power is supplied to an internal PC or workstation and how the components are powered.

Now, because computers are in this continuous state of power, heat problems can cause many issues. And so for this reason, computers have cooling devices such as fans and other types of component devices which allow the components to be kept cool and not overheat. Computer cooling devices such as fans are used to keep the components cool, but there's also other types of components such as the Heatsink, which is a fan directly above the CPU. Because the CPU is processing intense calculations, it needs to be cooled down. And so this dedicated device, known as a Heatsink, allows for the cooling down of the CPU. And then there's also other types of cooling, such as liquid cooling. And this has become a popular alternative to fans.

Now in order for the hardware to interact and operate on top of software, firmware is used. Firmware is data that is stored on hardware devices which provide instructions with how devices should operate. So firmware acts as the medium between hardware devices and software. All right. So now that we have this basic idea of internal computing. Ah, let's actually take a look at my own PC and identify the components we just listed off.

Demo of Hardware Components in

Here is my PC tower. Let's go ahead and open it up and look at the internal components of this PC tower as a heads up. If you have researched or built your own computer before, my cable management is not that good. So just a heads up there. Make fun of me all you want. But that is the case right now with this PC desktop. So let's go ahead and open this up. When opening up this PC desktop, we can see that there are a lot of wires here as well as some internal components.

The first thing that probably stands out to you is the heat sink. Unfortunately, we are not going to be able to look at the CPU because the heat sink has a paste between the CPU chip and this fan here, this unit. Which means if you pull it apart, you have to reapply the thermal paste. So for now, we're just going to say the CPU is under here and then this is the heat sink. Here is the graphics processing unit, also known as a GPU. So this is the card that will allow you to generate 3D and 2D images much quicker.

Down below here, this black unit is a power supply, so this converts the AC power into DC, allowing for all of the components to get power. And then behind here, which is a little hard to see for this setup, you can see that there is a black little board here with a whole bunch of different little components and this is called the motherboard. So the motherboard is what gives power to all of these components up here. You can see that there is a fan. This fan came with the PC tower and it is installed right here, which then you hook it up to the motherboard and then back here, if you can see we have two small chips or little cards here. And this is known and called the Ram. So this is where the ram resides. There is two chips or two cards here in particular for this setup, for this particular case setup,

The hard drive resides on the other side. I have a hard disk, hard drive that is used to store my data. And there's also an option for SSD which I do not have in this setup. This is an overview of the internal devices which reside when we open up a PC tower and we can identify the different types of components, they usually look pretty similar to this. They're very dependent on the model, make and model and the build.

Data Storage Devices

Let's go ahead and talk about the different types of computer data storage utilized in computers. So computer data storage is the recording or storing of information into a storage medium or device. Now, storing data is a core component of modern computing, allowing us users to store, use and manipulate data on a storage device. Now in data storage, there are two types of devices: volatile and non-volatile. Volatile is when power is off, data is lost and non-volatile is when power is off.

Data is kept on the device. It's important to distinguish the different types of computing or storage devices which allow for volatile or non-volatile. Now, when it comes to data storage, we have three primary types: local storage, local network storage, and then we have cloud storage. Hardware components such as Ram hard drives, solid state drives, optical drives, flash drives. These are all known as local or physical storage devices, which are able to be accessed by a common user like you and I. These different types of components are examples of local storage devices.

Now there's also local network storage, which is dedicated file storage, enabling different types of users and clients to retrieve data from a centralized device on a network. Most commonly, there is a network attached storage device, and these are devices and file servers, which are common devices used for local network storage. So what happens here in this particular case is that we have some users who are all on the same network and there is a Nas device that is set up on that network. When a user wants to get a file from the Nas device, this could be anything from a marketing spreadsheet to anything of general purpose of a company.

Let's just say they pull from the Nas device and users can continue to do this as long as they are all on the same network. Lastly, we have cloud storage. Now cloud storage is where data is stored on servers owned by other hosting companies. Cloud storage enables you to access data whenever you have an internet connection. So as long as you have an Internet connection, you can store files on servers and you can go ahead and pull those files whenever you want to. So these are the three primary types of storage that we can use as users. Oftentimes, they're either using local storage, such as using a hard drive or SSD, or you are using cloud storage like Google Drive, for instance.

Software

Software resides above the hardware layer. Now software is a set of instructions and data telling the computer how to work. Applications in programs are created and used to make computers usable. Without software, computers would not provide a relevant use today. Now, to start with the software chapter, let's go ahead and overview some well known layers of software. And to begin, we will overview operating systems.

Operating Systems Act as the interface between hardware and applications. An operating system is a core set of software used to communicate with other devices, hardware OS, handle the input and output of devices and really are the interface between hardware and software. There are different types of operating systems and these can include workstation mobile devices and server distributions.

Examples of workstation include Microsoft Windows 10, macOS or Linux, something you're probably very familiar with mobile devices, Android and iOS and server distributions such as Microsoft Windows Server and Linux server distributions On top of operating systems. We have applications. Application software is designed for end users like you and I to use. Examples of applications could include your favorite music player such as Spotify or any browser that you use.

Now applications have a few models used for delivery. There are applications locally installed which do not have network connectivity. So think of these as most likely applications on your desktop, which are used just locally. There's also applications locally installed on a hosted network which need a network connection, but the internet access is not required. So an example of hosted networks delivery could be a business or corporation who hosts applications on their local network and the employees can gain access to these applications. And then there can be applications delivered by the cloud model.

These applications require Internet access and the files are saved to remote servers. So as you can see, these are very similarly aligned with what we just talked about in the computer data storage chapter. So there's different types of storage and there are also different types of application delivery models. Now applications enable us to create useful and meaningful data. And in order to store this data, applications use databases. Databases are used everywhere to store data. This data can be in the form of employee records, personal information, inventory, customer profile information, passwords, accounting information, and much, much more. Now there are different types of database models, and we're going to go over the three primary ones, starting with structured data, a database that is structured conforms to a relationship between rows and columns.

You can think of this as a Microsoft Excel file where you have data in the cells with columns and rows. A database which has unstructured data does not have an apparent relational model like the row and columns in a structured database model. Common examples of unstructured data include audio files, chapter files and rich media, which just don't have that apparent relational model. And then we have a database containing a semi-structured data model, which is a form of structured data which does not conform to the formal structure of data associated within a relationship.

This is a structured database, but it doesn't conform again to that relational model of rows and columns. In this chapter, I quickly overview software, including different types of software and we use this to include operating systems which interact between hardware and software applications. And then we have applications on top of operating systems which allow us to create meaningful data and use these software programs. And then we have that meaningful data stored in databases and this is where that information is stored. So now that we have the very basics of hardware and software overviewed, it's time to start learning about computer networks.

Computer Networks and Networking

Computer networks enable communications across the world and understanding the function of computer networking, we are able to successfully establish what we know as the Internet today. In this chapter, we will be reviewing several important concepts to keep in mind in regards to computer networks. So to start off, what is a computer network also referred to as networking?

Well, a network is a group of two or more computer systems or computing devices that are linked together to exchange data by connecting two or more devices together, networks enable the capabilities to share resources, transfer files and really communicate over an electronic medium Networks can differ in type, but really all you need is two or more devices to make a computer network.

Now, in terms of types, let's go ahead and overview some popular types of networks, starting with the local area network, also known as a LAN. Now a LAN is a computer network which interconnects other computers and computing devices together in a limited area. Now, this limited area can be at residence, a cafe, a university, a library and most commonly known to you, your home network. So your home network is referred to as a LAN. A LAN spans across a relatively small geographical area or location.

Now, most lans consist of connected workstations and personal computers where each device has its own functionalities and is most likely communicating to the outside internet. But really, these devices can access each other's information locally on the network. So, for instance, this PC here can interact with this cell phone or this laptop if they would want to. But in most cases you're connecting to web pages and browsing outside the LAN. Now, two or more devices is considered a LAN, and you just need two devices to create this LAN. Now, connecting, transferring and communicating with other devices on a computer. LAN is able to communicate with local devices. But what if we want to communicate with devices or servers outside of your LAN?

Well, this is where a wan comes in. A Wan is a wide area network, so a wan spans across a large geographical area or location. And to do this really a wan connects two or more lans together. So what we know as the internet today is one big wan. It connects these small local area networks together. And what this consists of is one big Wan. The next type of network we're going to talk about is a virtual local area network, also known as LAN. Virtual local area networks are the logical groupings of workstations, servers and other computing devices which appear to be on the same LAN, but do not necessarily have to be geographically located in the same place.

VLANs are used to increase network performance, ease network administration and apply appropriate security controls in a business. So you will often see VLANs utilized in a corporate setting for these use cases because a corporate setting or corporate IT infrastructure has a lot of different computing machines and considering the scale and complexity of their IT infrastructure, VLANs can help categorize this data. So as you can see here, we have PC A and LAN Network A and PCB in LAN Network B Now let's just say that these are located in two completely different geographical locations. Maybe one is in the eastern side of the United States and one is in the western side of the states or even in the world. Right.

Well, we can create a Vlan, we'll call this Vlan one in this case. And as you can see, PC A and PCB can be under this Vlan. So let's say when you apply a password length requirement on these PCs to be more than 12 characters, you wouldn't have to go into each individual PC. You could just go to the Vlan, apply the appropriate security policy, and then it would apply to both PC A and PCB, which are located on two geographical different locations. All right. So now that we know what Vlan is, let's go ahead and go to VPN, which is a virtual private network.

Now, maybe you've heard of a VPN before. A VPN extends a private secure network across a public one. So VPNs provide services for both individual users and corporations by securing communications over the wire through encryption. And we'll talk about encryption, But the basis behind encryption is obfuscation or making information unreadable. So here, as you can see, we have devices on LAN Network A, and they want to communicate with this web server, let's say, in a completely different geographical place.

We can use a VPN connection which is first going to connect to a VPN server and from that VPN server then it can connect to the web server And in this case the connection now acts like it is coming from the VPN server instead of the LAN network. At least it appears that way. And in addition to appearing that way, VPNs also have encrypted tunnels, so VPNs implement both security and privacy depending on what you're looking for. Because in terms of privacy, it looks like the connection is coming from the VPN server to the Web server instead of a LAN network. So now that we have this behind us, let's go ahead and talk about two basic identifiers for network devices, also known as IPS and Mac addresses.

MAC and IP Addresses

In Mac addresses are unique identifiers which allow a device to be uniquely identified and connected to a network. So before we continue our networking chapter, I thought it was a good idea to go ahead and include this and we'll actually go over the IP and Mac address structures in future chapters. But for now I want to quickly define what each of these are.

Both Mac addresses and IP addresses are used to uniquely identify a computing or computer device. Mac addresses are used to identify a local machine, whereas an IP address is used to a device connected to a network. So to get started, let's go ahead and look at Mac addresses. Mac Address stands for Media Access Control. Now a mac address ensures that each device has a physical address. So as you can see, a mac address appears to look like the one in front of me here.

Now it is 12 characters long and we'll actually go through this in a future chapter. But right now I know that our Mac address is used to uniquely identify a device. Next is an IP address. IP stands for Internet protocol. Now, IP addresses are provided by Internet service providers or ISPs. IP addresses are used when connecting devices to a network, so when you want to connect a device to the network and identify the device, you can use an IP address. So an IP address looks like the one in the following below, separated by four dots.

This is known as an IP version four and we'll go over different types of versions of IP addresses in a future chapter. So Mac and

IP addresses provide the basis for how devices communicate with each other. And now that we know the very basis behind a mac and IP address, we can finally overview some popular network devices and equipment which allows us to enable communications across two separate LANs or networks.

Network Devices

Network devices are electronic devices required for communication of devices in a computer network. Now, network devices include a broad range of equipment and different types of functionalities. In this chapter, I'm going to go ahead and overview some of the most popular types of network equipment to be familiar with and to what they do as their functionalities. So let's go ahead and start with servers and clients.

Servers are computing devices on a network which manage network resources and provide functionality for other programs or devices. Now servers are often dedicated devices, meaning that they perform the tasks they're intended to perform, and no other task is to really be performed except those specific tasks. Now, a common misconception is that servers are remarkably different from our personal computers. And although there are several differences between a server and a personal computer, servers ultimately function in the same way as a personal computer.

Now servers provide various types of functionalities known as services. These services can be used by clients, which could be you and I. It could be someone else across the world. And the different types of server services include different types of database servers, file print servers, web servers, game servers and applications. Let's say we are on our favorite browser and we want to navigate to our favorite website. We type in the domain name or the little address there and we click enter.

What is happening in this case? Well, in the most high-level overview, we are creating a web page from a web server located somewhere around the world, and then we are able to get that web page which is then displayed through our browser.

Now this web page and all of its contents are hosted up on a web server. So I can go ahead and query for a web page in the United States and maybe you are across the world and you can query for the same web page located maybe on the same web server, depending on how big the website is. So that is the basis behind how servers work. The next type of network equipment is hubs, so hubs provide a connection point for devices on a LAN network when a data packet arrives at a hub. The hub shares the packet to all devices connected to that hub, meaning all devices are able to see the packet. So in this case, let's say we have five different workstations on a LAN network all connected to a centralized hub through an Ethernet cable.

When a data packet arrives from the Internet, it's going to forward all the data packets to the hub. The next type of network equipment is a switch, so a switch is similar to a hub in that it sends packets to devices on a LAN network, except this time a switch only forwards data to devices that need to receive it, meaning that a switch does not share packets across all devices. Data packets are forwarded to only one device, so this is considered to be a more secure solution than a hub, because if, let's say, an attacker were to be on the network, they couldn't just see a data packet being sent because it's a 1 to 1 data packet or only the devices which are intended to see that data packet receive it.

Next device is a router. Now you've probably heard of a router before. If you have a home network, a router is a device which forwards data packets along networks. So routers enable communication between networks while the networks remain independent of each other. Data packets are transmitted across routers until the packet arrives at the right destination. So in this case, if we have a LAN network and we have another LAN network, we can go ahead and use a router which is going to act as the intermediary device between the two networks and it will allow for communications between these two networks.

The next is the access point. So access points are hardware or oftentimes computer software, which act as a communication hub for users on a wireless device. So access points can be standalone devices or they can be integrated within the router itself. Oftentimes if you're in a home network, access points are automatically in the router itself. Now if you are in a big area, for instance, at a university, you're going to have different hardware access points set up across the university and these access points will forward the connection to the wireless router next is a modem. So modems are devices or programs which enable computers to transmit data. Now modems are usually used to connect across telephone lines or cable lines. So if you are in a LAN network and you have a home router, in this case, what will happen is the router will usually be connected to a modem.

Now the modem is going to transmit or send that data across a telephone line oftentimes through your internet service. Provider and it's going to actually provide you that Internet service. And finally, lastly, we have firewalls. Now, firewalls are systems designed to prevent unauthorized access coming from or to a private network. Firewalls can be hardware that can be software or they can be both. Now, we will be covering the different types of firewalls in the preceding chapters where we talk about the different types of defenses presented to us in cyber security. Right now, just think of a firewall is a way to prevent access from the Internet into a LAN or a different

network.

So these are some of the most significant and important network devices to be aware of when it comes to connecting devices to a network. Each has its own set of functionalities and being aware of what they do is important. So now that we have that in mind, let's go ahead and overview data communications through the TCP IP model.

The TCP/IP Model

Data communications is the transfer and reception of data over an electronic communications channel. When browsing over your favorite websites, it's seemingly easy. Experience from our point of view has an entered layer, a complex process working underneath. This Interlayer process works effectively to gather all information to enable efficient communication among devices.

The process of data communication connects many processes together, although the end goal is achieved in a matter of seconds. This process of data communication is really divided into layers for better understanding by network cybersecurity and general IT professionals. This layered process is commonly referred to as the TCP IP model. It is a standard for data communications. Now the TCP IP model specifies how data communications should be packetized, addressed, transmitted, routed and received.

The TCP IP model allows for the flow of data to be transmitted with the end to end principle. End to end Communication is a design framework used for communications of application specific features to reside on the end devices like my personal computer and not intermediary devices such as a router which establish the path in connection for the end devices to communicate with. The TCP IP model is divided into four layers where each layer has its own scope process and contains all related communication protocols. The TCP IP model is divided into four layers, where each layer has its own scope processes and contains all related communication protocols.

A communication protocol is a system of rules which allow for two or more devices to transmit information among each other. Protocols can be hardware, software or both. The TCP IP model defines different types of related communication protocols according to the scope of each network layer involved. So there's four layers in the TCP IP model, and this includes the network access, internet, transport and application layer. Let's briefly overview and describe more detail on the layers of each, starting with Layer one, the network access or link layer. So the network access or link layer establishes physical connection for data remaining in a single segment of the network.

Local hosts can communicate with each other without traversing through an intermediary device such as a router. Layer two is the Internet layer. This is going to be providing the internet working or using intermediary devices routers to connect two or more independent networks together. Next layer is transport. This establishes basic data channels for application use. So this is going to establish the basic connectivity to form what we know as the end to end principle or the end to end message transfer. And finally, we have the application layer and this is the process to process data exchange, to transfer application data over the network connection, providing user services. So this example could be a web page, a file transfer, email or more.

This is all going to be delivered on the application layer. The combination in internet workings of all four layers is what enables you to receive your favorite news and entertainment websites. The TCP IP model provides a conceptual foundation for how devices should communicate with each other. It's a layered approach where really each layer focuses on a core set of functionalities within its layer. Now, after roughly ten years of its publication, a new model was developed and published, and this model was referred to as the Open Systems interconnection model, commonly referred to as the OSI model.

In the next chapter, we're going to be breaking down the TCP IP model into more layers with the OSI model. And this is really where we learn about how each of these layers work. I just wanted to briefly overview what TCP IP was.

The OSI Model

The OSA model is an abstract model divided into seven layers similar to the TCP IP model. Each layer defines a set of communication protocols. The OSI model had been introduced. TCP IP network enabled devices had come into widespread use, so big companies had already made a significant investment in TCP IP network technologies, but the OSI model did not lose its relevance.

In fact, the model clearly defines how networks and protocols function with each other. The little model is theoretical. Concepts are regularly used to describe the operations of real world networks. And this is why, in addition to the TCP IP model, the OSI model is referred to and taught within the industry. The OSI model is divided into seven layers. Each layer still corresponds to the TCP IP model, but is further broken down into three additional parts.

The seven layers of the OSI model include the following. Physical data link network transport session presentation and application. Let's go ahead and overview each of the seven layers, starting with Layer one, the physical layer. Layer one Physical. So this layer is the physical equipment involved in data transfer. Physical equipment could be switches and cables, for example. The equipment is responsible for converting data into a bit stream of binary or strings of ones and zeros. Layer two Data Link. The data link layer facilitates data transfer between two devices on the same local network.

The data being transferred between two local devices is called a frame. The data is responsible for flow control and error control within the same network. Layer three is the network layer. The network layer is responsible for transmitting data across two different networks. The network layer sends data through units called packets, so the network layer is responsible for finding the best physical path for data to reach its destination. Layer four is transport. Transport provides the end to end communication between two devices.

The transport layer takes in data and breaks it up into segments. Segments are sent to the receiving devices to be reassembled. The transport layer is responsible for flow and error control. Layer five is the session layer. The session layer opens and closes communications between two devices. This layer ensures the session stays open long enough for all data to be exchanged, then closes those sessions when communication is finished. Layer six is a presentation.

The presentation layer is responsible for preparing data for presentation, making the data Representable for applications to consume. Examples of a presentation layer include encryption or the compression of data. In addition to these functions, the presentation layer also translates data. Because data is encoded in different types of formats. And finally, layer seven is the application layer. This is the layer which end users such as you and I interact with. The application layer is responsible for initiating communications. This layer is not to be confused with client software applications.

The application layer is responsible for protocols of communication, which a software relies on to present meaningful data. So think of a web page. So those are the seven layers of the OSI model, being familiar with which type of communications you're dealing with regarding each layer is going to help network professionals and cybersecurity professionals identify and troubleshoot any particular problem. Now, the TCP, IP and OSI model work from a bottom to top, top to bottom exchange, meaning that when a sender device sends data, it starts from the bottom up. And when the receiver device receives the data, it is processed from the top down. So that is how the TCP, IP and OSI models work.

Next layer we're going to be defining what a communication protocol is. Something that I have been throwing around there. We may not know exactly what communication protocol is. We're actually going to define some different types of communication protocols within the OSI model, the ones that to be familiar with.

Network Protocols

Now that we know the basis behind each of the layers and what they deal with, let's go ahead and overview the communication protocols that are defined in each layer, and I'm going to be reviewing the most important ones to be aware of in regards to considering cybersecurity, as I referred to previously, a communications protocol is a set of rules which define how devices will transmit information to each other.

A protocol defines a set of rules, syntax synchronization and error recovery methods to allow data transmission. Now these protocols can be hardware, software or combined together. Each communication protocol has a set scope and purpose. I want to overview some of the most popular types of communication protocols. We will be using the OSI model as a reference for which layer each of the communication protocols works in. Let's go ahead and start with layer two. Since Layer one deals with physical cables such as Ethernet cables and crossover cables. So the layer two or data link layer in regards to the OSI model has a couple of communication protocols to be aware of. This includes the Mac and the address resolution protocol.

So the Mac layer, something that we've actually already referred to as the Mac address is part of the layer two communication protocols. So the Mac layer operates on layer two and it is responsible for frame recognition, addressing for destination frame checking and control across a physical transmission. So the Mac layer gives the Mac address its functionality, meaning that it will send frames to each device located on the LAN network. Next is ARP or address resolution protocol. And this is used to discover Mac addresses given a certain IP address. So think of this as converting a mac address into an IP address or vice versa, because as we have noted that a device both has a mac address and an IP address, data coming in from the internet will be addressed through the IP address, not through the Mac address.

So in this case, what address resolution protocol will do is convert or discover the given Mac address, given the IP address or vice versa. Next is layer three technologies. In layer three. We have a couple that I want to introduce, and this includes the IP protocol as well as network address translation. So the IP protocol is an IP address and this allows for the internetworking between different devices, as I've noted before. IP addresses are used to enable internetworking between different devices. Internetworking is a process of connecting multiple computer networks together.

Now IP addresses are used to deliver packets from a source host to a destination host, given a specific IP address. IP addresses come in two different versions IPv4 and IPv6. IPv4 addresses are 32 bit addresses, something that we've seen before. And IPv6 is a 128 bit address. Now each bit can either be a one or a zero, and we're not going to get too far into this. But right now, just know that there are two different types of IP addresses. Now, because there is a depletion or shortage of IPv4 addresses, IPV six was created and launched in 2011. Now, the reason why we are still using IPv4 is because the industry has yet to change or to massively adopt the IPv6 addresses. So this is why sometimes you'll see both, sometimes you'll only see one, which is the IPv4 address.

Next is Nat or network address translation. And this conserves the IP addresses. Now, because IPv4 addresses had a depletion or limited amount of addresses, network address translation was created. So Nat allows an entire LAN to use one IP address when leaving the local network. And this works through the use of public and private IP addresses. So in the LAN devices such as workstations, laptops, phones will be assigned a private IP address from the router when the packets leave the router.

The private IP addresses are converted into public IP addresses and the public IP address is usually just one IP address. So then it goes out to the network. It's the web page, for instance, and comes back through the private and sends that data to the specific private IP address that is used in a router oftentimes. So just the basics of what an IP protocol and Nat does in layer three. Next is layer four and there's two that we want to quickly introduce, and that is the TCP or transmission control protocol and UDP and the user datagram protocol.

Now the transmission control protocol is a reliable order and has error checking. Involving reliability works through what is known as the three way handshake. The sender client receives a message or a synchronized message to the receiver, which is the server. The receiver sends a syn acknowledged message or synchronizes acknowledge back to the receiver and then the sender receives an acknowledge message back. And this is known as a three way handshake. So it's going to provide a reliable order and has error checking involved.

Now the user datagram protocol is connectionless, which means it does not perform handshaking, meaning that packets are just continually delivered without a guarantee of the individual delivery of each packet. So error correction isn't involved. UDP is often suitable for purposes where error checking and correction is not necessary, so this could be a voice over IP application such as Skype or streaming of chapters such as live streaming, where performance means much more than reliability of the data. Next is Layer six.

I want to review TLS, which is transport layer security. So this is a cryptographic protocol designed to provide a means of secure communications. It is often used in web browsing, email clients in instant messaging, and then there's also SSL or secure sockets layer. Now, this is a deprecated protocol which is also used to secure links between computer networks. TLS is a successor, but you may still see the SSL or TLS together, so it's important to be aware of both. And then finally, for Layer seven, we have several communication protocols that I want to overview. And now I'm going to quickly go over these.

And what I want you to know in each of these communication protocols is the basic functionality. So dynamic host control protocol or Dhcp provides automatic or dynamic assignments of IP addresses. So when you are on a LAN network and you're configuring a new device and you just click the connect to Wi-Fi, well, what's happening there? Well, an IP address is automatically being assigned through Dhcp. So instead of statically or manually assigning an IP address to each network device, because oftentimes network devices disconnect and reconnect to different types of networks. Dhcp is used.

Next is the domain name system or DNS. This is used to associate a given IP address with a domain name. This could be anything from Yahoo.com to Cyber academy.org. That's a domain name. Now the domain name is converted into an IP address and the IP address is where that web server resides, the public IP address. Anyway, think of DNS as the conversion of those two. Next is Http and Https. Http is an application protocol used for transmitting web pages and it was designed for communication between a web browser and a web server. So what happens here is that it populates the web pages.

Now Https is an extension of Http and allows for secure communication over a computer network and is encrypted with TLS layer seven. Communication protocols include some email protocols, so we have post office protocol version three or Pop3. This is used by email clients to retrieve email from a mail server. We have a simple map transfer protocol and this is used to send electronic mail to a web server, Internet message access protocol or iMap. And this is used to retrieve email messages from a web server. And then finally, we have some other communication protocols, such as the Simple Network Management Protocol or SNMp, and this is used for collecting and organizing information on IP networks.

We have FTP or file transfer protocol. This allows for the transfer of computer files between a client and server or from different clients to each other. We have an Http protocol. This is network time protocol and this is used for clock synchronization between computers and IP networks, ensuring that each of the network devices has the correct time synced. And then finally, we have two remote connection protocols which allow us to establish a remote connection to and from computers. So in this case we have Telnet.

This is used for remote connection and is considered insecure. And then we have a secure shell or SSH, and this is used to establish a remote connection across an unsecure network so you can remote from a computer on one network into another using SSH. So now that we know some of the basic functionalities of what communication protocols are and some involved in each layer, we now can identify the different layers where communication is happening as well as what kind of communication protocol we are dealing with as cybersecurity professionals.

Intro to the Cloud

If you're familiar with anything technology, you've most likely heard of the cloud. Whether it's using a cloud, storing files in the cloud, cloud computing has been experiencing rapid growth within the last decade. As the industry continues to evolve, the use of cloud computing and its corresponding infrastructure will play a major role in all IT professions. It is important to be familiar with basic cloud terminologies, including what the cloud is, how the cloud works and why it's implemented.

In this chapter, I'm going to briefly overview the cloud and its corresponding technologies that surround the cloud. Now, before I talk about the cloud, allow me to quickly overview the history of it and the context of business. And this is in the traditional data center. The traditional IT environment used data centers as a means of using computing devices in storing data. Data centers were located on the company's property and were used to house computer systems and network infrastructure.

Any type of service from external IT applications to internal computers for employees were powered through the data center. Now, data centers were located on company property, and this is why it's referred to as an on premise data center or on premise environment. Now, as companies continue to expand their IT initiatives, the traditional on premise data centers are becoming a source of maintenance havoc and they're very costly to set up, use and manage. And so this is where the cloud came into the picture a decade or a little bit more than that ago. So what is the cloud?

Cloud computing is the use of computer systems and network infrastructure used without active management by a user or group of users. Cloud computing is essentially using or renting of other network infrastructure and computer systems stored in different geographical locations. To provide a quick example, right now you are using a personal computing device, think phone, tablet or computer to view this Book. Most likely your important files, such as text documents, photos and chapter games, are stored on this device.

Now you own and use this device, right? Well, in the cloud context, the use and storage of personal files would be on a device located somewhere else. You can use this device as if it was your own computer, but you do not have to worry about the physical hardware surrounding that device. This is virtually what the cloud comes down to. You use a set of applications or software and the cloud provider worries about the underlying IT infrastructure, which could include the equipment.

The cloud has a variety of service models providing access to different resources depending on the model. I will overview the three most important ones to be familiar with, although there are many service models out there and there's even more being developed probably at the time of recording this. So the three basic ones are infrastructure as a service platform, as a service and software as a service. Perhaps you've heard of maybe software as a service, the most popular type, but there also are other service models. So starting with infrastructure as a service, infrastructure as a service is the delivery of network infrastructure, including access to server, network equipment, storage and virtualization technologies.

Infrastructure as a service provides the same technologies and capabilities as an on premise data center without the need to physically maintain or manage the hardware. Users of infrastructure as a service are responsible for everything above the physical infrastructure. This includes the hosting of applications, installing the operating systems, data management and more. Next is platform as a service or pass. Now platform as a service is the delivery of certain software, which is then used to develop applications on top. So platform as a service provides the platform for software creation so software developers can focus on writing the application with code without having to worry about the underlying network platform service often offers access to operating systems, software updates and storage.

So really this allows developers just to focus on their job, develop the applications and not worry about the underlying platform. This is where the cloud provider can come in. The next is software as a service or SaaS. Software as a service is the delivery of software over the cloud. Now, SaaS uses the internet to deliver these applications. The majority of software as a service applications run directly through a web browser. SaaS provides the ability for individual users to simultaneously use an application without having to download and install the application on each individual computer so the licenses can be set out on different computers and you can use them virtually wherever you have an internet connection.

So these are the three service models and they act as the foundation of the cloud model. Each service model has its own separate layer. Meaning you don't have to stack one service model on top of another. Now, why has there been a mass adaptation of the cloud? What is making these companies and individuals move from the traditional data center to something like the cloud? Well, there are a couple of beneficial characteristics. The cloud aims to cut costs and help users focus on their core business needs without having a deep knowledge about the underlying infrastructure.

As companies grow their IT initiatives, having the opportunity for a service model allowing companies and users to focus on their end goal instead of having to worry about the infrastructure allows for better growth within that company. So the cloud offers several beneficial characteristics, including location independence. They don't have to be in one particular geographical location. Maintenance, performance, scalability and availability. All of these, including maintenance, performance, scalability and availability. We allow the cloud model to be adapted, right? So it's easier to maintain something that is opened up in the cloud.

Let's say for instance, you have a little machine and it's not configured correctly. You can literally just destroy it and start from a new base model and as well as when your product maybe gets used more and more, more users come to your product, well, that offers scalability and availability. So that's why the cloud is being offered. So this concludes the IT Fundamentals chapter. The next chapter, we're finally going to move into the different types of attacks used to steal sensitive information, disrupt business processes and alter data. So in the next chapter, chapter four, we'll be reviewing cybersecurity attacks.

[Hands-on Attack Scenario] Setting Up The Attack

All right, so in this luxury to go ahead and set up our attack scenario by installing a program called VirtualBox, which is going to allow us to install a virtual machine onto our devices, this virtual machine, also referred to as a VM, simulates a business workstation computer. And specifically, this is going to be David's computer, who is the financial analyst for the business of Devout, a merchandising company. So this VM will be a Windows 10 enterprise edition.

Let's go ahead and download a virtual box installer Windows 10 enterprise machine. We first need to make sure virtualization is turned on within our computers. CPU churn is sitting on. We first must enter the bios, which is a firmer program which provides settings to adjust operating system settings and also programs to enter the bios. We first must restart your computer. And before the login screen is, I'll put it to the screen, you must use a computer model issued hotkey to enter the bios. Once inside the bios, you can use the arrow keys to navigate around the menus until you find the virtualization tab. And then you have to ensure that this is enabled before you restart your computer.

Perform a simple Google search to find the hockey used. Enter the bios specific to your laptop or computer model. Usually, it's f one or two, but it can be different depending on the computer model you have. Once you have found this hotkey, look up how to turn on virtualization for your specific computer model. I have the Lenovo X1 Carbon six generation, so I'm going to go ahead and just look up Lenovo X1 Carbon. Jan. six. BIOS Hotkey hears that it's going to be F1 or F2 for the supply to get into the bios, so I'm going to supply both F1 enough to simultaneously. Next, let's go ahead and look up how to enable virtualization.

It appears I'm going to go to the Security tab once I'm in the bios and then go ahead and choose the Intel virtualization technology and enable that. All right. So here in front of me, I have my laptop restarting. I don't have a hardware recorder here, so I'm using the good old method of recording my screen. So here it says to interrupt press enter. So I'm going to go ahead and press enter there upon start-up in the menu here. We can see what we want to do. And in this case, we want to enter the bios setup. So we're going to press F1 during setup and there we go. All right. So at this point, we can go ahead and use the arrow keys to hover over to security. And down here, you're going to see a setting called virtualization.

Press enter upon here and here you can see Intel, our virtualization technology and also the other features I have for both of these enabled already. But you can go ahead and it will do it, maybe again a little different, depending on your hardware model. Oftentimes, in the bios, you will see a little keyboard shortcuts, which will allow you to save and exit. So in this case, mine is F10, so I'm going to go ahead and press F10. Then it's going to prompt me to save my configuration changes. Press enter. And now we have virtualization enabled with our computer. We're just going to go ahead and let it set up. And from here, we can go ahead and install the VirtualBox hypervisor.

Let's go ahead and install our first virtual environment to play around with different operating systems and machines. And we can do this through the use of VirtualBox. Also known as a hypervisor through the power of a hypervisor, we can play around with other operating systems such as Linux and other Windows 10 distributions. So in this case, let's go ahead and go to our browser here. If you are on a Windows or Mac machine and simply, we're going to look up a virtual box. Here we go ahead and go to downloads and you can supply which platform you want.

In this case, I am looking for windows, but if you are on OSX, you can choose windows or we can choose OSX. Once you have clicked Windows hosts, you're going to go ahead and click Save File. And I'm going to fast forward until this has completed installing. OK, it is finished installing. We can go ahead and open the file. Here we're just going to go ahead and go through the default setup wizard choosing next. Using the defaults, you can choose the options if you want. In this case, I'm going to go ahead and choose all of them, and I'm going to go ahead and click, Yes. And then go ahead and click install. This will take a few minutes. We're going to go ahead and allow this to be installed. OK, this has finished.

Now we can go ahead and click finish. And as you can see here, we now have Oracle VM VirtualBox. Download it on our machine. From here, we can go ahead and start creating new virtual machines. OK, so our next step is to go ahead and import our Windows 10 enterprise machine. In this case, it's going to be David's. Now, as you know, you've downloaded that over a file from Google Drive and keep in mind, it's roughly 10 gigabytes, so it is a lot of space. So up on Oracle VirtualBox, what you're going to see here is a whole bunch of VMS. Don't worry about this for now, you're just going to be completely blank. This is my home computer, so I have tons of VM turning right now.

If you go to file, you can go into import appliances and this is what we're going to go ahead and do. I'm going to go ahead and find this dot over file, and in this case, it's going to be under my standard attack scenario. So here it is. And you can go ahead and click open. We're going to go to the next one here that's imported and just keep everything the same. Go ahead and click import. And this will probably take roughly anywhere from five to 30 minutes so you can pause this chapter and continue on to chapters. OK, so now you're going to see in a tech scenario, VM popped up once the file has fully installed. Perfect.

Now all we need to do is click start and this will start our virtual machine. And then this will probably take around another five to eight minutes to fire up until you get into the login screen. All right. Next up is to go ahead and supply the password, which is supplied on the screen here or just the standard password. And you're going to go ahead and let this low until you get into the home screen. Depending on your virtual box settings, you may or may not have a full screen like you see in front of me now.

To enable this, it's very easy where you can go ahead and go. Do is go to devices and then you're going to click Insert Guest Additions CD image. And this is actually going to install an image onto this virtual machine. Go down to the folder icon here. And click this PC when you're going to see that the virtual box icon is here and you can go ahead and click the virtual box icon and then where you see that the virtual box windows editions go ahead and just double click this and this is going to run the installation wizard. Then you're going to go ahead and click. The defaults and install it. And then I'm going to ask you to reboot your machine, go ahead and click Finish. Reboot your machine and then you will likely have a full screen.

Types Of Attacks

In chapter four, I will be reviewing the different types of cybersecurity attacks, including why hackers attack in the first place and what kind of attacks and methodologies they use to break into business, corporate or home networks.

Let's go ahead and break down exactly what we'll be learning in this chapter. We're going to be going over four different types of attacks, including network, social engineering, physical and malware. Now, each attack has its own scope and attack scale, and we're going to be going over each of these. Let's go ahead and get started.

Why do hacker's attack?

Before reviewing the different types of attacks, I first want to address why it is that hackers hack. Now, hackers have various types of motives when it comes to probing for and conducting attacks against a network. Some are motivated by financial gains, while others want to steal sensitive information.

Depending on the hacker or the hacking group, organizations, both small and large, must have an active plan implemented to protect against the assortment of different groups. Generally, a hacker or hacking group has one or more of these motives, including financial gain, which could include theft of credit card information, payment details, or personally identifiable information. Maybe they're bored or they're curious about what their abilities can do. They want to make a statement or send a message to a particular corporation or group.

They want to steal sensitive and proprietary information, perhaps for a competitive advantage. Government espionage and secrets. Maybe you've heard of this on the news, on your local news about different types of government espionage campaigns going on, or they want to disrupt business processes for whatever reason. Now, the majority of hackers or hacking groups are motivated by financial incentives. Although government espionage is also a very relevant motive in today's world. So each of these motives will help us identify which types of hackers we're dealing with on our network and how we can prevent them from getting into or infiltrating the network.

Network Attacks

Start out with chapter four. Let's go ahead and overview. Network Attacks. Now a network attack refers to the attempt to gain unauthorized access to an organization's network to steal, alter or disrupt information and processes within the business or organization as a whole. Now, there are many different types of network attacks, and we're going to be going over some of the following listed in the screen here. So let's go ahead and get started by talking about DDoS or distributed denial of service DDoS attacks.

A denial of service attack is a type of attack used in which the threat seeks to make a machine a set of machines or an entire network resource unavailable to legitimate users by temporarily or indefinitely disrupting services of the hosts connected to the network. A denial of service attack is a single host machine or internet connection which seeks to disrupt the processes of a machine set of machines or a network. So this is referred to as a DDoS attack.

Now, on a larger scale, we have a distributed denial of service or distributed DDoS attack. Now this is very similar to a denial of service attack, except you could say it's on steroids. A DDoS attack has the same objective of a DDoS attack seeking to make a machine or a network of machines or services unavailable. However, a DDoS attack is when more than one machine is participating in the attack. Frequently, a DDoS attack involves an entire set of machines, often called bots, or a group of them called botnets, which set out to make a set of services, machines or an entire network unavailable.

The next type of attack is a man in the middle attack. As the name suggests, a man in the middle attack is when an attacker positions themselves between a network connection or a conversation. The connection is intercepted between the user or an application, or perhaps between two different users. Man in the middle attacks are typically used to eavesdrop on conversation or impersonate a trusted entity. The next is injection attacks, and there are multiple different types of injection attacks. We're going to be going over three of the most common ones, but you're going to see a lot of them out there. So an injection attack refers to supplying untrusted input into a program which then gets processed by the interpreter, causing an alteration of the execution within that program or application. Injection attacks are the number one Web application security risks.

Now, common examples of injection attacks, which you will see is what is referred to as cross-site scripting or XSS. So these enable an attacker to inject client side scripts into web pages and bypass access controls and allow for attackers to execute malicious scripts on behalf of the user. So the user browser will execute these scripts, which will allow the attacker to execute these scripts and alter what they were wanting to do in the first place. SQL injections allow an attacker to view sensitive information such as usernames, password, personally identifiable information within the database because they enter the SQL injections into input fields.

And then very loosely we have remote code execution or RCS, RCS access or manipulate a computer or application to run arbitrary code on behalf of the application. So arbitrary code is code that the attacker can run on his or her behalf without the authorization of the user or application. Next type is DNS poisoning. Now we've briefly covered what DNS is. DNS poisoning is a type of attack used to spoof DNS records and supply a fake website instead of the real website within the DNS record. So with the fake website information like passwords, banking information or more can be collected. It may look like a legitimate website, but when it gets redirected to a malicious website, you can have a login page and steal credentials. There are many types of different ways that you can impersonate the real type of website.

So here, as you can see, we have a DNS record with a sample website and the attacker changes the DNS record to redirect to a malicious Website.com and malicious Website.com is what is supplied Next is domain hijacking. Domain hijacking is the changing of the registration of the domain name. So each domain name is registered to a particular user or entity. So stealing the domain name can facilitate phishing scams, password theft, spam, and distribution of malware. So as you can see here, we can have a legitimate user who signs up for sample Website.com has the address and tells you when.

Domain will be assigned an expired. Well, the attacker can change the domain name registration, change the records, and this can facilitate different types of phishing scams and password theft. Next is Rogue Access Point. So this is when a wireless access point has been installed on a secure network without the authorization of the organization, administration or entity. Now, a rogue access point could lead to a lack of possible security measures which could expose sensitive information. Now, this can be installed by an attacker or an unaware employee who installs for enhanced network connection. Right. So an access point once again is going to get you a stronger Wi-Fi signal.

And what you can do is you can maybe install one on your behalf and that could leak sensitive company information if you're working at a company. Now, an attacker could do this to impersonate at the company access point and then gather sensitive information from there, which actually leads us into the evil twin attack. So the evil twin attack is a Wi-Fi access point, which has been set up to appear as a legitimate access point. And how this works is that it copies the ID of the legitimate access point. And this appears to be legitimate.

So here in front of me, you can see that we have the Ssid fruit tried company and we also have the ID fruit trade company with the legitimate router. Now when a user comes into the company, the attacker may be, let's just say, is out on the parking lot and has this access point available and the Ssid will be the same. The user is going to authenticate with the evil twin or the attacker-controlled one, which then can steal sensitive information such as login information, password credentials and other sensitive types of information.

The next type of attack is Mac and IP spoofing. Now we've overviewed what a mac and IP address are and you can actually use this to impersonate another person or have a sort of a hide your tracks. If you are performing malicious activity on a network, the Mac address can be changed even though it's hard coded within the network interface card. There are drivers which allow the Mac address to be changed and with the Mac address you could bypass access controls or you could even impersonate another network device to make it look like it came from a legitimate user.

Now it's the same with IP spoofing. You can modify the source IP address to hide the identity of the sender or impersonator. An IP spoofing often involves a technique used to invoke attacks under anonymity. So as you can see in the screen in front of us with the graphics, we have legitimate users with the Mac address and IP address, and the attacker uses these Mac or IP addresses to actually impersonate the legitimate user. So these are some of the most common types of network attacks we will see. This is a very brief overview of what different types of network attacks companies or organizations will face.

Social Engineering Attacks

For the next chapter, we are going to be talking about social engineering attacks. These are very powerful within the cybersecurity industry because they prey on human weakness instead of inherent technical flaws. So what is social engineering if you've never heard of it before? Well, social engineering is the art of manipulating people to give up confidential information through the human inclination of implicit trust. So this uses or exploits loosely human weaknesses. And this could be accomplished through trust, urgency, consensus, familiarity.

Now, social engineering is carried out in several different ways, and we're going to be talking about a couple or a few of the methods used within the industry. The first one and perhaps the most prevalent one you may have even heard of this before, is phishing. Now, phishing is a type of social engineering attack, and this is usually carried out by email. So this is a fraudulent attempt to obtain confidential information by disguising as a trusted entity. Now, within the phishing email, usually carried out by email, you're usually redirected to a fake website.

You are prompted to open a malicious file attachment, or you give up sensitive information. Phishing is a very powerful type of social engineering attack and one that is very prevalent within the industry today. Now to expand on phishing, there is spear phishing. Spear phishing are phishing attempts directed at specific individuals or companies. Spear phishing gathers and uses personal information when targeting their victims in order to increase a sense of trust while enhancing their probability of success. They could gather this information through company websites, social media posts, public records and more.

So in this example here we have a phishing email sent to high level executives of a company with a Microsoft document. And let's say this has some financial information for all the high level executives to take a look at. Well, when you look at it, there's a macro inside which allows you to gain access or harvest credentials for the attacker. Next is vishing. Fishing is phishing, except it is used on a phone. So the medium is being carried out through the phone. So using the same principles of social engineering, an adversary, an adversary will try to gain access to private, proprietary or financial information. So they may call you and say, Hey, I'm an employee for a free, tried company, I'm in the accounting department, can you please give me this banking information?

And if you're working for free and let's say it's a big company, maybe you give the information up. Finally, we have hoaxes. These are deception techniques used to masquerade the truth. Hoaxes often distort or completely make up an event likely to be to be believed as real. A hoax is used to frighten or mislead recipients into believing or performing some sort of action. So you may see hoaxes all the time, maybe carried out through phone email. Or you say you've won $1,500 or you've won this certain amount of prize, just click here to claim it.

And well, when that happens, you are actually redirected to a fake website and it's just a total hoax. In the next chapter, we're going to be talking about physical attacks. This is also another type of attack that a lot of the industry tends to overlook but is very important for corporations. So let's go ahead and overview physical attacks.

[Hands-on Attack Scenario] The Email & Initial Access

Located on the desktop, here is an email sent by the attacker impersonating the CEO of DBU dot company Taylor Sanders. The attacker has crafted Taylor sender's email address by viewing how other email addresses were sent and then going ahead and trying to basically craft one with a very basic format. So for instance, if it's Taylor Sanders at D-Wade outcome, maybe you do.

Sanders Taylor at DBU dot com as an impersonating message, but this is often a very trivial way of reaching out to a list of contacts, and oftentimes this can be caught by an email filter or gateway as they call them. So another possibility to email address spoof is through email headers. Email headers are small code snippets which contain information about the sender recipient in the email route. The attacker can modify these email headers so that the client software displays the fraudulent sender, a message appearing to come from the victim's email address.

Upon opening the email message, you will find some generic messaging related to the DBU merchandising company trying to establish a sense of familiarity and trustworthiness. With David, our financial analyst and the email body. You will see an urgent message from the CEO to take a look at a third party company who provides services to your company. Quick look and this provides the accounting department with all of its necessary financial software for your company. You need to visit QuickBooks website to view more information about some missed financial software.

Upgrade and download this software and you need to write a review back to the CFO with what your thoughts are on the new features included within the software program. With the time sensitive task in hand, David needs to urgently complete this task as soon as possible, so he goes over to a quick look dot com and then downloads the necessary software from the company. While it may appear that he's installing some new software from Quick Look, it's actually an attacker control website. The software package that David just downloaded is some bogus bloatware with a special payload inserted by the attacker.

This payload contains an exploit used to gain access to David's Windows 10 machine, and now the attacker has direct control over David's computer. So now the package has been installed and this establishes a connection to the attacker controlling the machine and the attacker can upload as special software into their next step. So this is all accomplished by what they call a command and control framework and are also referred to as a C2 framework. A C2 framework is used to control compromised machines. It is a set of software tools and exploits used to establish initial access and persistence with compromised machines, so the attacker is using a C2 framework to upload their next suite of software, which is already installed on David's machine in our case. This tool helped the attacker steal passwords to gain access to more user accounts within the company network.

Physical Attacks

In this chapter, we're going to be talking about physical attacks, an attribute that's often overlooked within the industry. It's an attack vector that we should be aware of as aspiring cybersecurity professionals or just people who are enthusiasts for cybersecurity. So when it comes to physical attacks, what are they? Well, they are intentional offensive actions aimed to gain unauthorized access to a physical asset.

Now, this could be network infrastructure, physical hardware, workstations, a data center office space for sensitive documents. And really what this is able to do is either you're able to destroy, expose, alter, disable, or ultimately steal information from a corporation, a company, an institution. So there are lots of different reasons why physical attacks are carried out. We're going to be overviewing some of the most popular types of physical attacks, starting with impersonation. So impersonation, as the name suggests, is an adversary successfully assuming the identity of a legitimate party.

Now, an example could be an individual who impersonates a building maintenance employee or just another employee of the company. Right? So if you have a big company, you probably are not going to know all your employees. So let's just say, you know, an employee comes in and it's an authorized employee and the fake employee comes in after that. Employee: Well, hey, you know, if they're dressed the same or if they're dressed as a maintenance worker, they will rely on the implicit human trust to just go ahead and walk into the company. Borders. Next is dumpster diving.

Dumpster diving, as the name suggests, is salvaging of discarded materials from their owners. So this could be through companies, so used by an adversary to collect useful information about the company. Dumpster diving can reveal sensitive information from documents, papers and filing. Now, the mitigation that a lot of companies have set in place is companies will often have shredder station bins where the company documents must be discarded throughout their policy. So a recovered document can reveal sensitive information about maybe an employee that they could use for a phishing attempt, a spear phishing attempt, or just gather that information.

Next, we have shoulder surfing. So this is used to obtain personal information such as passwords or pins while looking over the victim's shoulder, while the victim is, say, typing on a keyboard or entering their phone password. Now, shoulder surfing attacks can be either direct where information is obtained in real time by an adversary or recorded where information is obtained after later playback, an analysis of the device. So this could be a chapter camera. You station a chapter camera above the keyboard when an employee comes in, walks down and types in their password, you have their password now. So in this example here we have an employee typing and we can have a person looking over their shoulder from behind.

Next is tailgating. This is when an unauthorized person follows an authorized individual into a restricted area. Now, adversaries will impersonate a worker or an employee of the building. So oftentimes they'll use a combination of impersonation, shoulder surfing or maybe even tailgating to get into a company. The importance is getting into the company and preventing that as cybersecurity professionals. So here we have an employee who's walking in and the tailgating employee impersonator walks in with him, maybe wearing the same type of clothing and they can just walk in.

Overview of Malware

Malware is often generalized with the different types of attacks included within the cybersecurity industry. Perhaps you have heard of malware before. Depending on the type of attack, malware has different types of functionalities and purposes. Now what is malware? Malware is any type of software intentionally designed to be harmful or disruptive to a computer, a set of hosts, or an entire network?

Now malware comes in many different types, and maybe you've heard of some of these before, such as viruses or ransomware. We're going to be reviewing the following malware types within this chapter. Now, before we do that, we're actually going to go over how malware works in a very basic way. So in general, malware works by first infecting the target device, whether that's through clicking a link on a malicious site or a user inadvertently performs an action which causes malware to be downloaded. The first step of malware is to infect the device.

Once the device has been infected, the payload of the malware is inserted. Now the term payload is used to describe what the malware is doing, which could be including the damaging of the device, stealing confidential information or many other purposes as well. Now, after the payload has been inserted into the malware, then it will perform techniques, techniques either used to spread the malware, avoid detection or even just delete itself after it's accomplished its purpose. So with this being said, let's go ahead and overview some of the most common types of malware.

Starting with viruses. A computer virus is a software which, when executed, inserts itself by altering or modifying a computer functionality, application or set of programs. An application typically is triggered which enables the activation of the virus. Viruses can be self-replicating programs which will modify software without the consent of the user. Now a virus performs some type of harmful activity to infect the host, which could include stealing private information, slowing down the computer, intentionally corrupting data, displaying political humorous or threatening messages, sending spam from email or logging keystrokes. So there's all different types of purposes behind viruses.

The next is ransomware, something you've probably heard of if you're at all familiar with in the cybersecurity industry? Ransomware is a type of malware which locks down a system by encrypting a victim's files, making them inaccessible. Demands for a specified ransom payment must be met in order for the files to be decrypted by the attacker. Ransomware has become a huge trend in recent years and has posed a big risk to companies of all sizes, both public and private. Ransomware can be delivered in various amounts of ways.

Usually attacks are carried out by Trojans, seemingly innocent looking files which have malicious intent to infect a computer or network of computers. But this can also be used through phishing attempts and many other different ways. The ransom is usually demanded through the form of a digital currency or cryptocurrency, most commonly through Bitcoin, which makes the transactions difficult to trace back to the attacker. Ransomware is an evolving industry. It's pretty incredible to see the innovation that has happened throughout the last couple or few years in terms of getting companies to pay the ransom or shaming them when they do not pay the ransom. Now the next is Trojans. Trojan is any type of malware which appears to be innocent or harmless, but actually has a malicious purpose.

Trojans are often delivered through seemingly harmless email attachments, advertisements or software programs. Now, typically speaking, Trojans do not look for ways to self propagate or spread. The name Trojan comes from the ancient Greek story of the deceptive Trojan horse, which was used to defeat the city of Troy. Now, in this example in front of us, we have a Trojan with chapter editing software and the user downloads this chapter editing software for free. But included within this chapter editing software, which functions as intended, it installs a backdoor which the attacker controls. So the functionality is still the same.

It's still working, but there is now a backdoor installed. Next is keylogger. Now, as the name suggests, a keylogger is a program which could be hardware or software to capture and record keystrokes of a user who typically are unaware of their actions being monitored. Now Keyloggers are mostly used to steal private information such as username and passwords. Software based Keyloggers are computer programs designed to capture and store keystrokes, whereas hardware based keyloggers do not depend on any type of software being installed. These types of keyloggers usually appear to be like a USB converter or thumb drive. So here we are, we have a keylogger installed and you are going to Facebook, Instagram and you type in your username and your password and those keystrokes are then logged and sent to the attacker.

Next is bots and bots nets. We've actually reviewed this before. A bot is a computer which has been infected by malware and then can be controlled remotely by an attacker. Now this is commonly referred to as. A zombie and a botnet is a group of bots or zombies controlled by a command and control server. CNC or abbreviated as C2 server. Botnets can be used to steal data, send spam and most commonly are used to carry out or perform DDoS attacks against a set of hosts. Finally, we have a backdoor. Backdoors are methods or computer programs designed to bypass normal security measures and gain higher level access on a computer system, network or program.

Now backdoors can be used to steal confidential information and install additional malware. A backdoor can be embedded in an operating system, computer hardware, computer firmware, or a computer program. Don't necessarily mean it can be malicious. Sometimes manufacturers or vendors will integrate a backdoor so that a service provider or its users can reset forgotten passwords. So here in front of me, let's say a backdoor has been installed on this client device. There is usually a connection or reverse connection which will initiate a connection to the attacker machine where they can upload additional malware, steal sensitive information, perhaps get a screenshot or two of what's going on.

So now that we've overviewed the different types of attacks, including networks, social engineering and Of course physical and malware attacks, it's time to move on to the different defenses we can use to prevent and defend against each type of attack. As aspiring cybersecurity professionals or perhaps enthusiasts, it's important to know what is offered to us within the industry. There's not a one size fits all type of solution, so it is important to be familiar with general and advanced cybersecurity defenses.

[Hands-on Attack Scenario] The Attack - Gathering Passwords

Now that the malicious file has been downloaded onto David's machine, the attacker will take a look at the network computer and user account information on this machine. There are several different tools an attacker can use at their disposal. And in this particular case, the attacker wants to view local user information, including computer accounts on this machine.

It could be the possibility of a local administrator, which they could log into and then move into a more valuable workstation or machine such as a business server. One method to accomplish this attack is through what they call credential dumping, which attempts to gain login information by breaking password hashes. Now, you may be wondering what a password hash is? Well, hashing is the method of transformation on a clear text password.

Hashing is a one way function, meaning you can't reverse the function. So instead of storing a password in clear text on the computer, hashing will convert the password into a random sequence of characters. In order to generate the same sequence of characters, you must supply the correct password. A tool used to achieve credential dumping is called Mimikatz. Mimikatz can expose password hashes stored on a machine. Then those hashes can be copied and then exposed by a hash cracking tool.

You can use this supplied information to go ahead and log in as the user and password located on the desktop. Here is mimikatz. Now, in a real world scenario, an attacker would not install this directly onto a computer or desktop. This would be quickly prevented by antivirus software. In this case, it would be a microsoft defender, which is the built in AV software and it has been disabled in our environment. So in a real world scenario, the attacker would obfuscate or make the Mimikatz program unclear to the AV software so that it wouldn't recognize Mimikatz. This can be accomplished through string manipulation or changing the contents of Mimikatz to look like a real software program. But the underlying functionality is still the same.

For the sake of simplicity. I've disabled Microsoft Defender and downloaded Mimikatz directly onto the desktop. Let's gather all the usernames and passwords of this machine through the security account manager or Sam. Sam is the database used to store user accounts and security descriptors for users on the local computer in a Windows environment. So transitioning over to our virtual machine, this is where you can follow along within this exercise. As you can see here, Of course, we already have the Mimikatz program installed and like I've highlighted, this would be run in the background through the attacker controlled C2 framework.

For the time being. We are just going to keep this very simple and just say that this is where Mimikatz will be run. Our next order of action is to go ahead and get the security account manager files. In this case, there's going to be two. So let's go ahead and go over to our command prompt shortcut here.

We're going to right click it and run as an administrator and then go ahead and select. Yes. The command prompt allows us to interact with our file system similar to the way that you would act with the Windows Explorer here. So, you know, you usually interact with the desktop or maybe your downloads folder.

Well, in this case it's just a text way of doing it. So right now we're in C Windows System 32. Let's go ahead and grab these files. And in this case, I've looked up two that are of particular importance. And to do this, we're going to go ahead and proceed to go to that file location. So in this case, what we're going to do is supply CD space and then go ahead and supply the following file path. So it's going to be C colon backslash users David with a lowercase desktop and then go ahead and press enter as you see here on the screen.

Now we are into that file location. Perfect. Let's go ahead and supply our reg save command and get those two files that I talked about. So in this case, it's going to be Reg save, which is a registry command h com forward slash Sam. Sam. Backup HIV. You can see the operation has completed successfully. We're going to do the same for the second file. And you can pause this chapter and supply these if you want to, if you're following along. This case, it's going to be a system instead of Sam. And like I said, we're just going to hit enter and the operation has completed successfully. Now, as you can see, we have two files. Perfect. This is what we wanted to do. So for the time being, let's go ahead and exit out of our command prompt. And now we're ready to go into Mimikatz. Okay, so let's go to our Mimikatz icon here.

And again, we're going to right click on this case and go to run as administrator again. Choose. Yes. And here we have another command prompt, similar to the one that we just were interacting with. The first thing that we need to do is go ahead and elevate our privileges. To do this, we're going to go ahead and supply the following two commands. Perfect. So you're going to see two things. You're going to see a privilege. 20. Okay. And then this output here.

Next thing we want to do is go ahead and logout output, which is this output here onto a file. In this case, it's just going to be a simple text file so that we can go through it in a moment here and I'll show you what I mean. So just for right now, just do log hash dot txt. The last step we need to do is go ahead and supply this following command, which we'll go ahead and take a look at the system backup and the SAM file and see if we can get and crack those hashes or expose them to this. Do a dump, colon. Colon, Sam and then supply system backup HIV. And we can do the other file as well.

Hit enter and you're going to see all this output to our screen. That's perfect. And now we can go ahead and look through this output, either through our command prompt here or if we go to our text file. You're going to see it in our text file as well. And in this case, we're going to go ahead and look for two particular things in this file. All right. The first order of action is to go back to our desktop and right click and then select new. Tax documents and we can call this whatever. In this case, I'm just going to call this username. Dash hashes. We're going to go ahead and double click this to open it.

Now, we're going to go and do a little split screen here in this case. And the first thing we want to do is scroll all the way back up with our hash output. And so to look at this in a very basic sense, we can see that there is a username called Administrator Guest defaults and this WDR utility account, these are some of the default accounts that Windows supplies within their system. Now in addition to this, if we start scrolling down, you can see that we have a user called David Well, who we know, Of course, is our financial analyst. And here is a hash name and there's the following hash.

If we keep going down here, we can see that there is also another local user and in this case it's Jared Admin. So this isn't a default account supplied through the windows. This is one that we created. And as you can see, there is also another hash. Now if we go ahead and copy the following output and paste it. Into. Our file here and then press enter. We're going to go ahead and do this for the hash as well. And then go ahead and enter again. And we'll do this with Jared admin as well. Copy. And let's copy this here. Perfect. If you take a particular look at these hashes, you can see that they're exactly the same. So what this implies here, well, these could be the same passwords. But let's go a step further and actually see if these are passwords and if we can expose them. So let's save this file. And the next step is to go to our browser.

Now, I went ahead and bookmarked a resource onto our Firefox browser here, and in this case it's called Crack Station Online. This is a hash cracker. What we can do here is go ahead and add our hashes into this output box here. And we're just going to do both. Now, Of course, I'm thinking that these are going to be the same, but let's just see. Do enter. We want to make sure to supply these on different lines. Select " I'm not a robot and then go ahead and select the correct hashes. And as you can see here, it automatically identifies that these are hash types. And here is our password, which, Of course, you knew David's password, but we didn't know Jared's.

And we suggested that, well, it is the same. So in this case, an attacker could use the local admin account and perhaps move laterally, which means go into a different machine on the network and start doing the same process over and over again until they get to perhaps a more valuable resource such as a server. And the server could contain a database full of passwords or that could just lead into a whole nother level of triage. And that is the basis of the credential dumping attack, something that's super simple to do and yet very effective.

Types Of Defense

In chapter five, I will be overviewing the different types of defenses, including both general and advanced tools and technologies used to defend against active and passive cybersecurity attacks. Cybersecurity defenses are controls we can use to prevent, detect, mitigate and recover against malicious threat actors, attacks and vulnerabilities. Without appropriate defenses installed in our environment, we ultimately risk the chance of becoming breached.

Now, in this chapter, we're going to be talking about the following types of defenses, including an overview of general cybersecurity defenses. And then we're going to be going over some advanced defense technologies, including cybersecurity technologies and cybersecurity software. So let's go ahead and get started with the general cybersecurity defenses we can use.

General Cybersecurity Defenses

Now there isn't a category known as general cybersecurity defenses formerly within the industry, but I've titled this to reflect some common, well known types of cybersecurity defenses we can use. This category contains popular types of at home security tools that you and I can work with as individuals. I'm going to be reviewing the following different types of general defenses and just what they are exactly in terms of what they are. So let's go ahead and get started with antivirus.

Now, if you've used a computer before, you've likely heard of AV or antivirus software. AV software are programs used to prevent, detect and remove malware from a computer or device? AV has been used since the early 1990s and has evolved throughout the industry as it's grown now. AV works through identification and detection techniques. Once a malicious software has been identified, AV mitigates and prevents the program from being executed. Traditional AV relies heavily on signature based detection.

Signature based detection had to determine whether a program was malware by first being analyzed by malware researchers and analysis systems at the AV firm. If the program was determined to be malware, a signature file would be created and added to the signature database of the antivirus software. If the program was to be downloaded by devices using this AV software, the signature would prevent the program from being downloaded or executed. Now, even though the signature based detection techniques were largely effective at the time, malware authors were able to adapt by writing polymorphic malware, which are programs encrypted or able to disguise themselves and avoid the traditional signature based detection to catch up with malware authors.

And the game of cat and mouse and heuristic based approach was developed known as Next-Gen AV. Heuristic detection works through identifying the common behaviors in areas of all devices used. Once a baseline has been created, variants of malware can still be mitigated against because of their baseline behaviors. Next is MFA or multi-factor authentication. Multifactor authentication is an authentication method used to grant access after successfully presenting two or more pieces of evidence. MFA works by granting access after more than one piece of evidence is supplied.

Now the evidence can be in many different ways, so this could be something users know, such as a standard password, something the user has, such as a card or smart token. The user is such as a fingerprint where the user is, which relies on detecting users location or something the user does, such as performing a specific action. So here in front of me, we have two factors for multi factor authentication. We have the standard password and then a four digit code is sent to the individual after the password is applied. So it's multi-factor authentication. Next is encryption.

Encryption is the process of making plain readable text into unreadable text. In order to view this unreadable text, there must be a key used to decrypt the information. Now encryption is used in a wide variety of ways. Oftentimes we will see encryption used for data at rest and data in transit. Now data at rest is inactive data which is stored in encryption and can be used for the files. Data in transit is when data flows between public untrusted networks. So here in front of me we have plain text, which is Hello world. We apply an encryption key which then produces what they know as cipher text.

This is a string of characters which is unreadable, and then we can use the decryption key to decrypt and get the plain text message. Again, this is the way or the basis behind how encryption works. Next is password management. Password management can be achieved through ensuring all passwords. Meet a minimum length and complexity requirement. Passwords are generally considered strong if they meet a minimum length. Usually eight or more characters have a mixture of upper and lower case, a mixture of letters and numbers in at least one special character.

As the industry has continued to evolve, stronger passwords means more complexity leading to the forgotten password problem. And this is where password managers come in. Password managers generate and store passwords for a user. You must remember one very strong master password to access all passwords stored in the password vault. Next is data backups. Although backups may not appear to be the most sophisticated defense, it is a very important and necessary control to implement. As the name suggests, backups create a copy of data.

If the original data were to be damaged or disrupted in some way, the backup can serve as a way to restore the information. Now, in general, backups can be offline or online. Offline backups are backups which contain a copy of data and are stored offline or disconnected from the Internet. Online backups contain a copy of data which are accessible online. Now, offline backups provide additional safety through not changing data corruption or. Auction if accessed online backups provide more convenience and are easier to use when data needs to be restored. So oftentimes companies will combine both an offline and online backup plan where they have the baseline data in an offline, and then they can have the more recent updated data on an online backup.

Next is the general advice of staying updated. Keeping systems up to date may appear to be obvious, but is something not to be overlooked? Receiving the most recent updates on systems and programs ensures past vulnerability disclosures are patched on the system. When a system stops receiving updates and is beginning its end of life or EOL life cycle, it's important to start either phasing out the system or developing a strategy to mitigate future risks, such as disconnecting the entire system from the Internet. And then finally, there are firewalls. Something we've already talked about in this little Book.

A firewall is a system which monitors incoming and outgoing network traffic based on a set of rules. For right now, no, a firewall typically establishes a barrier between a trusted and untrusted network. Firewalls are often categorized into network or host based firewalls. Network firewalls filter traffic between networks and are run on network hardware. Host based firewalls run on a host computer and control network traffic coming into and out of the machine. Firewalls establish a barrier and provide an additional line of defense between a trusted private network and an untrusted public network. All right. Now that we've talked about some general cybersecurity defenses, let's go ahead and go over some cybersecurity technologies presented to us.

Defensive Cybersecurity Technologies

All right. So we're going to go ahead and go over some different types of cybersecurity technologies. Now, what is cybersecurity technology? They are a set of systems which work to prevent, detect, authorize, mitigate and recover against a set of threats, attacks and vulnerabilities. That is a loaded sentence there. There are all types of cybersecurity technologies used to serve various types of purposes, from wandering the network to authenticating user accounts and or ensuring the prevention of sensitive data not being stolen.

Cybersecurity technologies are used within different environments and may serve many different purposes. We're going to be reviewing some common types of technologies like the ones in front of us. And something to note is that in a company setting, they will use both these technologies and in addition, use the general cybersecurity defenses that we talked about in the previous chapter. All right. So let's go ahead and talk about virtual private networks.

A virtual private network establishes a protected, secure tunnel over an insecure public channel. This is something that we've talked about in the previous chapter. This can provide a secure connection for employees, contractors and individuals within a company. Now, there are often two types of VPNs used. One is remote access and the other is site to site. Remote access is where the location is changed frequently. So this is oftentimes used for traveling employees who will use remote access VPNs to authenticate into the headquarters. So as you can see, we have an employee in Europe, we have an employee in Asia, and they're going to use a VPN client to connect to the headquarters, which is located in the United States.

Next is site to site. This is a VPN which is set up in a fixed location. So oftentimes this connects branch offices together to a main office. So you can see Branch A and Branch B have VPN tunnels connected to the headquarters building and Branch A and B have a secure connection or tunnel established between them. Two. Next is a proxy. So a proxy is an application or hardware device, which acts as an intermediary device between two devices. It acts on behalf of the requesting client. Now proxies intercept connections between the client, evaluate the request and perform required network transactions.

Now, in corporate environments, proxies are added to add a layer of security, privacy and load balancing. Here in front of me, we have a client which is requesting a web page from a web server. The connection is first going to go through the proxy, which intercepts the connection and reads Where it's going can either block the connection, it can authorize the connection to the web server. So this is where a proxy can come in in a corporate environment. Next is an IDs intrusion detection system or IPS intrusion prevention system. IDs are network security technologies used to monitor and detect possible attacks and an IPS is an extension of an IDs by adding the ability to block threats in addition to detecting them. And these are considered in-band devices. So there are different types of IPS.

One is a signature based on an antivirus, which takes a sample of network traffic. If the network traffic suddenly changes, an IPS can take action and then there is heuristic based, which can intelligently look for or probe for malicious behavior from a program within the system. So as you can see in the examples in front of me, we have an IDs which is monitoring the connections between a local area network and the internet in between the router. And it can just detect any malicious behavior, but it can't act on that. So that's considered an out-of-band device.

An IPS is an in-demand device where in between the internet and the LAN, it can prevent a malicious connection being established from the internet or vice versa. Next is data loss prevention or DLP. DLP is used to ensure sensitive information. Confidential, proprietary or critical information does not leave the corporate network. Now the software detects blocks and reports, sensitive information or data trying to be sent out from the network. Often you see software on email gateways because email is used within a corporate setting. Here in front of me, we have an email containing basic information for an employee requesting a change in the bank information. It's really just an attacker for sending the email.

The DLP software intercepts reads and then prevents the email from leaving because it contains some common information such as the banking accounting number or routing information. And then finally, we have a CRM or a system information event management system. This is used to integrate network equipment into one centralized area. This organizes and prioritizes alerts for security teams to take action. So this keeps track of logs and generates useful alerts, dashboards and metrics so a security team can prioritize security alerts. Here in front of me, we have three different types of network equipment. We have IDs, we have a server and a firewall, and they all generate logs on a weekly, daily basis. Right. They're all going to be kind. Get it into the Sejm.

The Sejm is going to take a look at the logs. Look for some events that could provide greater insight into where to look into the network equipment and then provide priority for security teams to act on. So first it's going to be the IDs, then the server, then the firewall. All right. So these are some of the different types of cyber security technologies presented within the industry. And we're actually going to be going over some different types of cybersecurity software that we can use so that we can either detect or prevent attacks from happening.

Defensive Cybersecurity Software

For our next chapter, we're going to be reviewing some different types of cybersecurity software, both offensive and defensive tools that we can use. Cybersecurity software are tools used in cybersecurity to evaluate and manage various functions and test functionalities and different components of their corresponding environments. There are many different types of software tools and I want to overview some very common ones used throughout the industry, including the ones presented here on the screen. I'll start with packet analyzers.

Packet analyzers also referred to as protocol analyzers are used to capture and analyze data traffic as they traverse through the network. To accomplish this task, a packet analyzer intercepts network packets as they pass over the network and decode the packets. Raw data. Packet analyzers can be used for both malicious and legitimate uses, legitimate use cases or appropriate uses, including gathering the network packets for troubleshooting, gathering network statistics, monitoring network usage and analyzing network packets contents to see what is being leaked. Malicious uses could be for to spy on and collect sensitive information or to initiate a man in the middle attack.

Next is network scanners. Now network scanners are tools used to find and categorize devices running on a network. They return a list of devices running with their IP address and their associated services running on the device. They work by sending packets out to hosts on different network and the system will acknowledge the packet

and then reply with device information. Here in front of me, we have a network scanner, initiates three different scans to three different IP addresses. As you can see, two of the devices are using Windows 10, one of them is using Linux. So what we'll do is a network scanner will receive the IP addresses as well as the OS information and perhaps some other services that are running.

Next are password crackers. Password cracking tools are used to break and recover passwords. Now password cracking tools assist in the process of cracking by automatically applying a list of generated passwords to a user account. There are two general types of password cracking techniques. One is the brute force crack. This is a technique which uses computing resources or processes to guess the password in hopes of eventually guessing the correct one. So brute force is going to try every single combination of a password using computer resources. So it's going to start with a, then a, and then continue down.

A dictionary is kind of a subchapter of a brute force attack in that it uses a list of known passwords. And these lists are often compiled into a massive list of common passwords. A dictionary attack may include some main passwords and a supply. Those to the login prompt for a website. Next is vulnerability scanners. Vulnerability scanners are computer programs and applications designed to scan computer networks and applications for known vulnerabilities. These vulnerabilities have already been disclosed to the public, so it's already public information. These scanners will identify and then detect the vulnerabilities.

So as you can see, we have a vulnerability scanner which is going to go out into the environment and scan for different vulnerabilities on a web server, file server and workstation. The vulnerabilities can then be reported back to the vulnerability scanner with priority with which ones to remediate. And then finally, we have exploitation frameworks. Now exploitation frameworks are software packages which contain exploit chapters. What this means is that these frameworks allow you to use different exploit payloads against vulnerable systems, which then allow you to compromise a set of networks or a set of hosts. So here in front of me, we have an exploitation framework. This is a Metasploit command.

Actually, you can set the payload to a particular exploit. In this case, it's going to be Windows Meterpreter, reverse TCP and you can compromise the device. What this payload will do is actually create a shell within a Windows computer so that you can take a screenshot, you can perhaps steal data, upload files, upload malware. So it's an exploitation framework and this allows you to test for your different systems and compromise devices. All right. So now that we have a complete overview of cybersecurity defenses, including general techniques, tools and applications used to evaluate and defend against the different types of attacks, it's finally time to get into the practical side where we can apply the knowledge we've learned from this Book.

To do this, I'm going to be showing you how to set up a virtual lab hosted on either your very own computer right now or the use of a browser. So let's go ahead and transition into the final chapter of this Book. We're actually going to do some practical application and get away from just pure chapters.

Practical Guide

In chapter six, we are going to go ahead and get hands on. We've learned a lot in the past five chapters, including the different types of cybersecurity attacks and defenses. We are going to be working on a demo which you will be following along with, which is going to show the value of encryption and how it works. Now we're going to be using a packet analyzer, something that we've overviewed before as our tool to show how encryption works. So let's go ahead and get started.

Let's overview what we're going to be doing in this demo. We're gonna be downloading a popular packet analyzer known as Wireshark, and then we're going to be setting up a packet capture on Wireshark so that we can see the different types of packets traversing through the network. Then we're going to navigate to an Http and Https website. Then we're going to note the difference between the two. And really we're looking for encryption. Are we able to read the text? Before we get started, let's go ahead and do a quick review of what I have reviewed here, including what a packet analyzer is. So it is a software program used to capture and analyze data traffic as it traverses through the network, as we've overviewed previously.

What a packet analyzer will do. It will intercept the network packets traversing through the network and it will allow us to capture those packets. Now that leads us to packet capture. A packet capture intercepts a packet or groups of packets crossing over the network which is then stored in a file for later analysis. Now, in terms of protocols, what is Http? Well, it is a layer seven protocol as we have reviewed before in the OSI model, which is used to transmit web page documents and Https is an extension of Http where it's used for secure secure communication through encryption using the TLS protocol.

And then finally we have encryption that converts plain text into unreadable ciphertext. So we have a plain text password or maybe a plain text message saying Hello world, and we can convert it with an encryption key so that it's unreadable to the human eye as the internet has continued to progress. Http and Https have evolved. We're going to go over the quick history of Http and Https and more than likely you will see Https everywhere. Well, that wasn't the case at one point. And in this demo we're just going to be displaying why that is. Http was developed by Tim Berners-Lee and his team between 1989 and 1991, and Http was originally developed to exchange textual web documents or web pages, also known as HTML between clients and servers. In 1994, Http was extended to have a secure encrypted transmission through SSL 2.0 protocol known as Https.

So as e-commerce websites more specifically came to a rise in the Internet, there was a need to secure the credit card information, usernames, passwords and more. And in this case, there needed to be an encryption protocol used because Http sent its web page or textual documents in plain text. Now, Http had been in wide scale use by the time more websites had become available to the Internet. So Https wasn't widely adopted unless you were one of the big websites like Amazon. So over the years, especially within the last decade, since around 2012, there's been a huge initiative to enforce Https within all modern browsers for all websites. So if you are a user or you're an owner of a website, oftentimes you will be penalized in terms of search rankings if you don't have Https enabled.

There's been a huge wide adoption to extend Https life through Https and only use Https while querying for different web pages. So why are we going over something that has been widely replaced? Well, I want to show you the difference between how information is transmitted and how you are going to be doing this through a protocol analyzer. So what we're going to be doing in this tutorial or demo is we're going to be downloading Wireshark and we're going to see what kind of information is transmitted between an Http and an Https website and see the difference in terms of encryption.

Now, Wireshark is able to be downloaded on Windows, Mac and most Linux distributions. So with that being said, let's go ahead and get started by downloading Wireshark onto our desktop.

[Demo] Download Wireshark

Okay, so I've transitioned over to a Windows 10 environment. I'm going to be using Windows 10 to download Wireshark. But as I said or highlighted before, you can use Mac or Linux to go ahead and download Wireshark. So here in front of me, I've actually already pulled up the web page to download Wireshark. The URL is here. Just type that into your browser of choice and here in front of me, as you can see, we have the different types of download options and in this case we're going to go ahead and download the 64 bit version for Windows.

We'll go ahead and click Save File and we're just going to go ahead and use the standard process of downloading this client or software walking through the wizard. All right. It's finished downloading. I'm going to go ahead and click on it. All right. I've clicked on it. We're going to go ahead and click Yes. To allow the install. The wizard has popped up. We're going to use the defaults. So we're just going to click next and sign the agreement and just use all of the defaults.

We're going to allow this to be installed. This could take a couple of minutes. So I'm going to fast forward until I have the Wireshark software tool downloaded. Once the installation has completed, we can click next and just finish. Now, if we go ahead and use the search feature. As you can see, we have Wireshark up in our apps chapter. Awesome. So now that we have Wireshark open, we can go ahead and start a file capture.

[Demo] HTTP vs HTTPS - Encryption Demo

Now that we have Wireshark Open, it's time to test the difference between HTTP and HTTPS. Okay, so I have Wireshark open here, and you're going to see some lines here. This means the network interface. So you have different network interfaces depending on what your computer is connected to. If you have a direct Ethernet cable connected to your computer or desktop, you're going to use Ethernet. If not, if you're connected through a laptop, through wi-fi, then you can use the wi-fi. Here.

I have two sites: HTTPS website Wikipedia.org and a test website called Test PHP web Volcom, which lets us test the username and password fields for an HTTP website. Okay, so since I'm connected to Ethernet, I'm going to use the Ethernet interface. Up here, I'm going to click the start capturing packets, this little wire fin. Going to our browser, I'm going to create some dumb username and password. It doesn't matter what you put in here, you are going to see this little warning here. It says that our connection is not secure.

You can press the log in which will allow us to say, sign up or whatever. Just log into this. We don't need to save it for now. Going back. I'm going to pause this capture by clicking the pause square. And here, as you can see, we have our packets captured. Great. So now we can do some analysis within this Here. Do that. I'm going to go up to my little search icon here and put in HTP. And then enter. Now we are going to look for the HTTP post request. So there's different types of HTTP methods, as they call them.

Others the git method, then those the post method. In this case there's a few others. I'm not going to go over them for the sake of brevity for this Book, but I'm going to go ahead and choose the post. And the reason why I'm choosing the post is to get. As you can probably tell, we'll get information from a page post. We'll post content to that page. Clicking this packet CAPTCHA. Here we can see our IP address followed by the IP address of this web server. Right clicking.

Going to follow the TCP stream. You will see a whole bunch of information now in this case. There really isn't much to look at except for looking at our host this test php of home webcam. And then as you can see here, you name equals Buddha password equals this right here. Now can you believe that at one point in the internet we were sending, you know, HTTP passwords and usernames in clear text. If we close this, go up to file.

Save as let's go to this desktop title it h t http dot. P cap and then save. Going back up to our file. Let's close this. And we're back to our home screen. Now let's see https. So if we go ahead and click our Ethernet network adapter again. Go to. Firefox. Here I have my login page on wikipedia. Password you want. You don't have to have an account. Click log in. Since we don't have an account with that, that is okay. Go to Wireshark. We're going to pause the packet capture and right now we have nothing. And that's because we have this little filter applied. Go to the little X to click that out. And already you're going to see something that's a little different. If we type in HTTP followed by Enter, we get nothing. And the reason that that is happening is because we are using HTTPS, which uses TLS. So going back up to our little square here.

You're going to see all kinds of different things, different packets. We can click any of these TLS 1.3 packets here. Let's click this one which says application data. Right click.

Follow the TCP stream as we did before, and everything is encrypted from top to bottom so that in this case we can't get any information on where this user went. We have no idea that they went to Wikipedia in this case because it's encrypted and it's just a blob of messy text. This is the difference between HTTP and HTTPS. It's pretty incredible to think that not too long ago, a few decades ago, most of the Internet traffic was running on HTTP. And, you know, you could send your clear username and passwords in clear plain text across the network.

Practical Application in Cybersecurity

Packet analysis and Wireshark are just one of many tools used within the cybersecurity industry. Learning how to practically apply abstract concepts into real world uses is imperative when developing cybersecurity skills. As with any new skill learned, you must first understand the abstract terms and concepts in order to actually practically apply your knowledge.

Now, in this Book, we've managed to overview many useful and important terms and concepts related to general IT and cybersecurity. But the journey does not stop here. If you're interested in developing more practical hands-on skills while also learning more about the concepts involved and covered throughout this Book, then I have a resource for you now. Due to the scope of this Book, we did not cover in depth concepts and also have a ton of hands-on learning, but this resource does the following.

It adds a more in depth approach to cybersecurity while providing hands-on projects. In this Book, you will learn how to set up your own cybersecurity, home lab or lab environment through virtualization, you're going to develop a small scale simulated business network, learn how to work with Linux, a popular operating system in the IT industry, learn how to use shell scripts, work with and configure the Linux firewall and also have a hands on practical application with Python through developing real world scripts while also receiving a complete introduction to general IT and cyber concepts. In this Book we will review cybersecurity domains IT fundamentals, networking IT, security fundamentals, Linux programming and then we finally do a launching into your own learning journey where I provide a ton of resources for you to get started.

Now, in addition to each of the following chapters, I also provide a learning resource in a complete 30 plus project list document so that you can expand upon what you've learned within this Book. So if you're looking for a more in-depth, hands on and complete resource to get started, I do have this 15.5 plus hour Book available to you now because you're in this Book. I want to provide a discount for you using the code in the screen below or intro Book you all caps in the promo box. We will provide a 33% discount upon checkout. There is absolutely no pressure just telling you about this resource for you if you enjoy this type Of course, and my teaching style and you want to continue your learning journey.

Conclusion - Where to Go Next?

We have successfully completed the complete introduction to cyber security Book. In this Book, you learn the very basics of cyber security. Hopefully you have found this Book useful and very resourceful for you. And thank you for taking this Book. And if you're interested in your own learning journey, you can follow me in the following handles on the screen here.

Again, thank you very much and I hope that you have found this resource and Book useful for you and best of luck on your learning journey. If you have any questions, please do not hesitate to reach out to me. Thank you and have a good one.

Understanding Society Sociology for Everyone An Accessible Social Science

Sociology is the scientific study of human society and social behavior. This Book is designed to introduce you to the fundamental concepts, theories, and methods of sociology and provide an understanding of the complex social structures and processes that shape our lives.

Throughout this Book, you will explore various topics such as social stratification, inequality, social institutions and processes, globalization, and social change. You will also learn about the different theoretical perspectives in sociology and how they are applied to analyze and explain social phenomena.

By the end of this Book, you will have gained a deep understanding of the central concepts and theories of sociology and their relevance to real-world issues. You will be able to apply your knowledge to analyze and understand social issues and to think critically about the world around you.

Who This Book Is For

1. This Book is suitable for anyone who is interested in understanding the world around them through a sociological lens.
2. It is particularly beneficial for students who are majoring in sociology, social sciences, or related fields, but it can also be taken as an elective Book by students in other majors.

How Does Our Social Environment Affect Us?

Social environment. We as humans can do extraordinary things, we can speak, write, read, build skyscrapers, travel to space, predict natural phenomena and countless more. What makes us so different from other species? In this chapter, we will answer this question. A big part of our accomplishments can be credited to our ability to learn. Our ability to learn enables us to understand new information, gain knowledge and adopt new behaviors. But this capacity is not only limited to us, other species also exhibit the ability to learn behaviors like those that we perform.

For example, chimpanzees have been taught to work a food dispensing machine. They learn to get food by inserting poker chips into the proper slots to distinguish different sizes and colors, to use each chimp in the appropriate opening and, where necessary, to insert two chimps. Nonetheless, the apes are incapable of learning to perform the vast majority of behaviors we perform in our everyday lives. An example of this is that apes cannot learn a language.

Therefore, we can conclude that even though both humans and apes can learn to act in certain ways, the degree to which they can do so has a substantial and great significance. Why can't apes learn more complex behaviors? Is it because of their hereditary features or is it because they are exposed to a different environment than we humans are? What would happen if an ape was raised by humans? Would it be able to adopt complex behaviors?

To answer this question, a couple of researchers perform the following experiment. For a short amount of time, alongside their son, they raised a female chimpanzee. Both the chimpanzee and their son were younger than one year old at the time. Both were treated with the same kind of care. They ate, slept and played together. The chimpanzee being stronger and physically more mature than their son, was naturally more adept at motor activities such as climbing and acrobatics.

She also showed greater speed of movement. More interesting, the ape very readily learned some of the so-called humanizing behavior of which the child is capable. She learned to eat adroitly with a spoon, to drink liquids out of a glass, to skip rope, to open doors. Indeed, she learned to do these things better than their son and in general was more cooperative and obedient. But in respect to the crucial matter of speech, she lagged behind. The ape came to comprehend a large number of words and phrases, but she never learned to speak.

We can therefore assume that the inability to learn complex behaviors, such as using human language, was not due to her social environment. But the limitation was inborn. Their son, Of course, learned in the customary manner of children. This is the case because humans have the inborn capacity to learn speech. This is, in fact, only one of the many skills humans can learn.

We don't know the complete limits to our inborn learning ability. We may yet learn to do many more extraordinary things in the future. This simple experiment revealed that hereditary features have a significant impact on what one can comprehend and learn when exposed to a rich social environment. On the flip side, what happens if someone is gifted with the ability to learn complex behaviors but the environment doesn't foster learning those behaviors? In other words, does our upbringing and social environment influence the expression of our inborn gifts? To answer this question, we may look into how people that were unfortunate enough to be raised among animals, away from human beings, adapt to the human environment when they enter civilization.

In some cases, they retain their animal-like habits. They eat raw meat and walk on all fours. They gradually, with a lot of care from others, learn to abandon these behaviors. But they tend to lag in learning to speak or they make no progress in this department whatsoever. If we assume that no mental deficiency was present at birth, it becomes evidence that our inborn capacity to learn does not unfold itself, but must be developed by our parents, our peers, our teachers or some other stimulus of our social environment. Let's summarize what we discussed in this chapter.

We are capable of extraordinary things. This is in part due to our hereditary features. We have the inborn ability to understand new information, gain knowledge and adopt new complex behaviors. A prime example of this capacity is that we learn to communicate with others using language. At the same time, our social environment plays a big part in the development of our inborn gifts. Without social groups to help us unravel our inborn abilities, we would never accomplish much. Therefore, both our hereditary features and our social environment have great significance, the combination of these to give us the characteristics that differentiate us from other animals.

What Is Culture And How It Influences Us?

Culture. By being around other people, we have plenty of opportunities to learn. There are customs institutions, books and various types of associations. Our environment is enriched with science, tools, art, religion and more. This rich and varied environment is what we call culture. In this chapter, we will learn about culture and its significant impact on us.

We can understand the impact of culture by contrasting it to our natural environment. Our natural environment consists of the earth, sun, sky, water, trees, plants and other animals. It is very important for our survival, but the vast majority of the things we know, we have learned in our social environment. For instance, in the Mississippi Valley, the natural environment was the same in the 20th century as it was in the 17th century. Yet children growing up in this natural environment in the two periods would learn quite differently. In the earlier period, a child would learn to hunt, to fish, to trap, to gather different kinds of herbs.

He would believe in mystical powers. His language would be Indian. He could not read or write and would not know how to drive an automobile or how to play baseball. In the 20th century, the young person probably learns English and the Christian religion. His moral conduct is different. He learns perhaps the art of salesmanship or the operation of intricate machines. He knows nothing about how to trap and little about woodcraft. But he may learn much about music and painting.

What individuals do and what they learn will vary for two different cultures, even though the natural environment is the same for both. Apart from the different skills that we learn, depending on our culture, we also may be more or less likely to experience particular emotions. For instance, some cultures are more optimistic than others. In others, there may be an attitude of despair. For example, people that live in poverty are more prone to stress and depression. Our cultural environment also affects our predisposition towards some personality characteristics. For example, a culture may discipline youth strictly as in ancient Sparta.

In this culture, children would be more self disciplined. On the contrary, cultures that allow children to grow up with scarcely any discipline at all as a New Guinea encourages self-expression. All things considered, what we learn and who we become depends upon the particular social environment into which we are born. The type of life we follow is likely to be set for us by the particular culture we share. Let's revisit the key points of this chapter. Our culture encompasses the characteristics of knowledge of a group of people. In today's day and age our culture is rich and varied.

Our culture stands in stark contrast to our natural environment. The latter is important for our survival. But it is our social environment that enriches our lives. Even in the same natural environment, two cultures can be vastly different. Our culture affects what skills and beliefs we adopt, defines our language as well as our art and recreational activities. It sets up expectations as to how we should behave and what personality characteristics we should adopt. It also affects what emotions we experience. All things considered, our culture has a major impact on our lives.

What Is The Role Of The Social Group?

Social group. From the moment we are born, we need protection and attention from others. Without them, we wouldn't survive. Thus, it doesn't come as a surprise that living with others is an indispensable part of our lives. What functions does group life fulfill for us? This is the question we will answer in this chapter.

What is a social group?

It is a sum of people that interact with each other, and while they do so, they share a sense of unity. Such groups are families, circles of friends, companies, clubs and religious congregations, among others. What impact do these groups have on us? Firstly, they give us our culture. This is the case because social groups are to a large extent responsible for transmitting the social heritage. As children, we begin to acquire the culture through our family group.

Later, the neighborhood playgroups and the school assists the family in this function of familiarizing us with the objects, the ideas and the values of our culture. Two groups are not the same in our complex and rapidly changing culture. These groups and consequently the social heritage they pass to their members vary significantly. What we learn depends on the particular family we are raised and the special groups we later identify with. For instance, someone who was raised in the country will be different from someone who is raised in a big city.

Therefore, in a complex culture such as ours, groups are selective instruments. They determine what aspects and versions of culture we acquire. Secondly, group life also shapes the personality of the individual. Whether a person is a leader or a follower, cooperative or competitive, social or unsocial may depend on his or her experiences in groups. For instance, a boy brought up in a small family will be different from a boy reared in a large family, and both will be unlike a boy who grew up in an institution.

Moreover, all these boys will behave differently in their homes from the way they behave in the schoolroom, and in neither place will they act as if they do at a football game. These adjustments to their behavior will be due to the control that the group exerts over them. Being part of a group requires one to conform to its norms. By belonging to a group we quickly learn that the opinion of others is very important. No matter if we are in Melanesia or in America, not respecting the rights and opinions of others will make our life uncomfortable. Thus, we are likely to conform by changing our physical appearance the way we talk to our habits and more. As part of the group, we usually also conform to certain patterns.

For instance, we follow the leader of the group and depending on the group, we cooperate or compete with our associates. These dynamic patterns of human interaction called social processes, are vital factors in the shaping of our personality social groups. While they transmit the culture and shape our personality are also themselves shaped by the culture. For instance, groups may exercise control in democratic or dictatorial ways. They may praise conflict or they may praise peace.

This is due to the fact that some cultures have institutions, either economic or military, that are highly competitive, while other cultures seem to encourage cooperative practices. Let's summarize what we learned in this chapter. A social group is a sum of people that share a sense of unity. Social groups have great significance for us. They give us our culture. They do so while being selective instruments of the aspects and versions of culture they pass to their members.

They also shape our personality by exerting control over us. As a result, because we fear rejection from them, we tend to conform to their norms. At the same time, we also follow the social processes of the group. Social groups affect us, but they are also affected by the culture. Understanding the various types of groups and social processes is essential in order to fully understand human experience.

What Are The Origins Of Our Culture?

Origins of culture. We can find culture everywhere from our museums full of paintings and sculptures to symphony orchestras playing music to libraries containing thousands Of courses. Magnificent as these marvels are, they constitute only a small fraction of our modern social heritage. How did culture begin to grow to become so complex and diverse as it is today?

What mechanism facilitated it? These are the questions we will answer in this chapter. We can define culture as behavior that is passed through learning from one generation to the other. Culture is dependent on our ability to learn and share ideas. Therefore, without the ability to learn from each other, there is no culture. Since learning is so important for the transmission of culture, we need to understand it further. What is the origin of learning? In the beginning of animal life on the planet there was no learning.

The behavior of animals was a simple response to stimuli, and it still is for the most part. For instance, a moth sees a bright light and is automatically drawn to it. The light is the stimulus and the moth's movement toward it is the response. No one taught the moth to go towards the light. Its behavior was due to an inherited mechanism. Thus, its action is an instinctive behavior controlled by heredity. Animals can even exhibit complex behavioral patterns instinctively. For instance, mother cats bring the prey they hunted back to their kittens and drop it to be eaten all by instinct.

Gradually, animals develop the capacity to learn not only through experience, by responding to environmental stimuli, but also systematically from those of their own kind through imitation and communication, for example, certain social animals seem to exhibit some behaviors which young learn by imitation. These behaviors include methods of hunting and of stampede, as well as some slight modifications of fighting and sex behaviors. For instance, mother cats teach their kittens how to catch mice and rats.

If the mother cat kills rats in the presence of her kitten before they are four months old, her kittens are almost twice as likely to develop into rat killers. Kittens raised with rats as companions killed none of them, nor any of their kind. Thus, learning plays a large part in determining whether a kitten will be a rat killer. Not all animals can learn through imitation and communication. Their capacity to learn is a function of the physiology system, especially the nerves and their organization. Therefore, the more elaborate the nervous system, the greater is its capacity to learn. The monkeys and apes learn best of all, though, elephants, horses and dogs also have great capacity to learn.

In the case of humans, our behavior is both determined by heredity and by learning from the social group. For example, heredity contributes to such behavior as sucking, swallowing and blinking, while behavior like talking English, wearing clothes and driving a car is learned from others. A factor with a great influence in the development of our culture is our ability to communicate through speech, even though from the beginning of the animal world, animals could exercise social learning, the absence of speech set limits to what they could learn. The ability to speak and understand a language was the big event that helped to make our culture so magnificent.

Why was language so important? A highly developed language gave us the opportunity to convey ideas about a tremendous variety of things. For instance, transmitting an idea such as the flood came and destroyed the houses was an achievement far superior to the transmission of states of emotion by a small variety of cries. At the same time, a language also perpetuates knowledge over many generations. Gradually, with the development of language, we also developed inventions and cultural traits to accommodate our needs.

Therefore, starting hundreds of thousands of years ago with sticks and stones, humans have achieved the amazing technology and social organization we now enjoy. Let's revisit what we discussed in this chapter. With the transmission of behavior by learning and especially by established learning through the group, our culture starts to develop. All the marvelous things our culture encompasses would be impossible if there were no transmission by learning, if the only transmission were by heredity.

Animals usually instinctively respond to environmental stimuli, but similarly to us, they can also learn through imitation and communication. Their ability to do so depends on how elaborate their nervous system is. Our behavior is the result of instincts and learning from a social group. A very significant skill we learn from the social group is the ability to speak a language. By doing so, we can share ideas and pass knowledge to the next generations, thus our opportunities to enrich our cultural compounds.

Is Our Culture Biologically Determined?

Culture and biology. Does our inherited nature dictate our culture? In this chapter, we will explore the relation of culture to our biological nature. Suppose you visit a hospital with newborn infants from various places of the world. Would you be able to predict what type of family they would form as adults simply by looking at their anatomy? Probably not. What if you were to run psychological tests on their behavior? Again probably you wouldn't receive an indicative answer.

Suppose now that you know in what family they will grow up, as well as what type of families their culture approves of. These might be monogamous families, polyamorous and polygamous ones, family systems with and without divorce, families with concubinage, large family systems and small family systems. With this information available, you are now much more likely to reliably predict his or her future family type. We can therefore conclude that once culture determines the particular social organization of the family, not our inherited nature. Generally our inherited disposition gives us a general direction to the shape of our culture.

For instance, our sexual nature seems to indicate that there would be some kind of organization of behavior around sexual activities. Thus, our nature indicates broad trends. But the dictation is not invariable as to detail. If culture were a direct expression of our biological nature, then culture would be in complete harmony with biological nature. But evidence shows that there are many customs that are contradictory to our biological needs. In our culture for instance, the bearing of children when the mother is young, yet mature is biologically appropriate.

Yet many women postpone marriage or bearing children until late in life, well past the best biological period. They do this for various cultural considerations, for instance, to focus on their career. The best biological age for marriage does not coincide with the best cultural age. Factors that influence what our inherited nature and culture dictates are our learning and discipline. The more learning there is, the greater the chance for disciplining or modifying the natural expression of our biological impulses. Culture also sets up different customs regarding our biological behavior. Customs are types of behavior that are organized and repetitive in a particular culture with the intention of regulating our biological activities and dictating how we will behave.

Customs form around a variety of activities such as marriage, birth, trade, production, and art. Particularly binding are the more customs that are regarded as essential to group welfare. These types of customs set the tone for what is considered morally acceptable within the particular society. For instance, one would hardly advocate that democracy is not the best type of government without raising suspicion of others. Of course, customs and mores might change in the Book of time.

What is deemed right at one time may be deemed wrong at another in the same society. And what is right at one time may be wrong at another. For instance, the mores make slavery wrong today, yet in the past they made slavery right. Let's summarize what we learned in this chapter. Our inherited disposition gives a general direction to how our culture is shaped, but it does not dictate it.

Culture consists of an order of phenomena that are different from our inherited nature and goes its way with a certain amount of independence from it. Our culture might modify and set limits to our natural impulses. When we live in a culture that encourages learning and discipline, we are more likely to act against our natural disposition. Cultures use customs and mores to control our behavior. Customs regulate our behavior and mores, set the tone for what is considered morally acceptable. With time, they might change.

Why Do We Form Groups?

Group life. Other people play a vital part in our lives. They give us our culture and they shape our personality, we would all be different than we are if we lived in a different group or in no group at all. Since the group has such great significance for us in this chapter, we explore in more detail its role on human experience. Belonging in groups is something that we enjoy doing.

Is it because we inherit a disposition to live in groups, or is the explanation to be found elsewhere? There is no proof that we have an inborn tendency to live with others. It's characteristic that the newborn baby shows no preference toward his own mother. His main drive is to satisfy his organic needs. The baby is absolutely dependent on outside assistance to help him meet those needs in order to secure his survival. It is this dependence that constitutes the primary reason for group life, thus, as he grows up, he learns that adults fulfill his needs and he tends to favor them.

It is interesting to note that infants below six months of age smile only towards adults. They don't seem to care about being with other children. When other children are present, they usually simply disregard them at six months of age. There may be a brief period of touching, but even at a somewhat older age, children do not appear to enjoy each other's company as they grow older. Children begin to appreciate the fact that more and more pleasures are possible only in groups. A boy cannot play baseball by himself with time.

Children understand that numerous satisfactions are enjoyed in and through groups. Therefore, human association becomes a source of enjoyment in itself. We like to be with others and we feel lonely and uneasy when deprived of human contact for any length of time. Acceptance by the group becomes a source of the greatest pleasure and rejection by the group, the basis for the most severe mental anguish. Although human life is full of group experience, not all groups hold the same degree of significance for us.

Groups are meaningful in accordance to what they do for us. For instance, our family is a significant group for us. A group with much less importance is strangers we come across when visiting a busy street. An important question to answer at this point is do we and the strangers constitute a social group? The answer is yes. Whenever two or more individuals come together and influence one another, they constitute a social group. So although we may not talk to anyone, although we may indeed feel lonely and strange, we will at least have to take others into account as we walk our way through the maze.

We have little to no common interests with those on the street, but we still influence each other, even if it is not in a substantial way. As our experience suggests, some social groups are more important to us than others. Which groups hold the greatest significance for most people? These groups are our family and friend groups. These groups are referred to as primary groups and they are characterized by intimate association and cooperation. During this association, there is a certain fusion of individuals in a common whole in order to align with the common life and purpose of the group.

We learn how to discipline ourselves, how to feel sympathy for others, and how to pursue mutual passions. As a result, primary groups are fundamental in forming our social nature and our ideals. This is especially true during infancy and early childhood, when primary groups have a great bearing upon personality development. It is important to note that we can form groups even with people that we don't share direct face to face association with. Such direct contact is not essential as long as we have developed a level of intimacy with them.

For instance, we might make friends online even if we haven't met with them. We can still develop a relationship with all the essential significance of a primary group experience. The opposite is also true. We might have face to face interactions with someone and not experience any intimacy. For instance, even married couples might feel that they don't really know their partner. We now know that our family is a primary group, what type of group is the group we form with strangers on the street that we previously discussed?

This is a secondary group. The characteristic of this type of group is that it is lacking intimacy. Such groups are educational groups, political groups, athletic clubs and the church, among others. Usually when we participate in such groups, we experience indirect contact with others. For instance, we might work from home without ever meeting our colleagues, but we still belong in the same group. Secondary groups might also be impersonal.

For instance, a college student sees and hears the chapter, but he may never get to know him. In this case, there is direct contact, but it is impersonal. Nonetheless, in both cases, there is no intimacy between the members of the group. Let's review what we learned in this chapter. Social groups play a vital role in human experience. We don't inherit a disposition to live in groups, but from the moment we are born, we depend on others. Later, we understand that more and more pleasures are possible only in groups.

As a result, human association becomes a source of enjoyment in itself. Some groups, such as family and friends, have great significance for us. Such groups are referred to as primary groups and are characterized by intimacy and cooperation. Primary groups greatly affect our personality development and teach us various skills. Secondary groups are less significant for us. The members of these groups lack intimacy and they experience impersonal and indirect contacts.

Do We Alter Our Behavior When We Are Part Of A Group?

Behavior in groups. Do we modify our behavior in order to be part of a group? Does the group deliberately control our behavior? These are the questions we will answer in this chapter. Depending on how important a particular group is to us we are more or less inclined to be loyal towards that group. If we value it we tend to be kindly disposed toward those whom we identify with in our own group.

We treat them sympathetically with something of the personal touch. We are sensitive to one another's opinions. We seek to win group approval and to avoid group disapproval. Therefore, we are eager to change our behavior in order to be accepted. As a result, we can conclude that group relations are effective influences on personality because of the pressure they exert.

To what extent do we feel that we need to change ourselves or in other words, conform to be part of the group? To answer this question, researchers performed various experiments. In one experiment, they tried to find out if and how much we alter our judgment simply by belonging to a group. To test this idea, they presented the subjects of the study with 10 different odors. Their task was to rate each odor. But what makes this study interesting is that the participants would rate the odors, both apart from and in the presence of a group of other participants.

When they rated the odors alone, their judgments were more extreme. The unpleasant odors were judged to be very unpleasant and the pleasant odor very pleasant. When they were asked to evaluate the odors in the presence of a group, their judgments were more moderate. Therefore, the effect of the group was to cut off extreme judgments, suggesting that the group exerts a restraining or conservative influence on human behavior. In this experiment, the participants, just by virtue of belonging in a group, decided to express conservative judgments.

What if they knew what the opinion of the majority of the group was on a subject? Would they adopt that opinion? A rather simple experiment revealed the answer to these questions. The participants of the experiment were asked to make judgments in the fields of morals by indicating which of two ethical choices they regarded as less offensive. For example, disloyalty to friends or cheating on exams. After making their choices, they were informed as to the majority opinion of the group, and they were retested.

As you might expect, there was a swing away from their original answers, and they exhibited a greater degree of conformity to the majority opinion. Therefore, we can conclude that by belonging in a group, we let go of our standpoints and we are more inclined to adopt the opinion of the majority of the group. This adjustment to our standpoints most of the time is done automatically and at an unconscious level, and it is only a small part of the changes we make in our behavior.

As a part of the group, we usually make a lot of adjustments because by interacting with others we are always subject to social pressure. What is social pressure? It is the pressure that is used by our society to regulate the conduct of its members. Furthermore, it comprises its system of social control and it is used to maintain order. In smaller societies, the means by which social pressure gains effectiveness are public opinion and gossip. Usually in these societies, order is preserved without the need for a constituted authority, since individuals have their behavior regulated automatically by unformulated social pressure.

This is the case because in these societies the group is the best of disciplinarians. The group is frequently able to exert more effective control over the conduct of its members than can an outside individual charged with special authority. As a rule, the most efficient regulator of all is a group of people of the same age and interests. For instance, a child might have a serious disciplinary problem, but when being in the presence of other children, he is more likely to give up his antagonistic ways and conform to the group because he doesn't want them to dislike him.

Informal social pressure is effective when we have a small, homogenous, relatively stable group where each individual is sensitive to the opinion of the others. Is it still effective in large, heterogeneous or rapidly changing groups? In a large community like a modern city, contacts tend to be impersonal and escape into anonymity is possible. At the same time, cities are composed of diverse individuals who might hold conflicting moral standards. Thus, under these circumstances, gossip is a less effective instrument of social control. Therefore, formal and organized instruments are required for adequate social control. These formal instruments are predominantly the laws, the police and the courts.

Let's summarize what we learned in this chapter. When we are kindly disposed towards a group, we care about its members and we are sensitive to their opinion. We seek approval of the group and we tend to modify our behavior and opinions in order to be accepted. As experiments revealed, we adopt conservative standpoints and conform to the majority opinion. Usually these changes are done automatically and at an unconscious level. When interacting with others, we are subject to social pressure, which is used to regulate conduct in small, homogeneous groups where each individual is sensitive to the opinion of others.

Public opinion and gossip are an effective means of regulating behavior. On the contrary, in large communities where contacts are impersonal, gossip is a less effective instrument of social control. Thus constituted authorities are responsible for regulating the conduct of the members of the community.

What Is Status And How Is It Determined?

Social status. The aristocratic classes in many countries where work is considered to be menial would rather be poor than risk the loss of status that would result from going to work. This illustrates how acutely humanity feels about rank and position. Since status is so prominent in our society, it is worth inquiring what status is, how it is acquired and how different groups, namely social classes, vary in respect to it. These are some of the fundamental matters we will illustrate in this chapter.

What is social status? The simplest definition of social status is that it represents the position of the individual in the group. A person's status is his group standing or ranking in relation to others. Thus, we say that a person has a high or low status in the group, that he is a leader or a follower. If one has a high social status, he is perceived to be competent in a way that facilitates the group. Therefore, he is more likely to be respected and honored by his fellow group members.

At the same time, status also conveys the idea of formalized behavior of some sort. The leader makes plans, issues, orders and makes sure that they are carried out. He has certain functions to perform a definite role to play. Behavior associated with a particular status is what we refer to as a role. A person's role in the group is the dynamic aspect of his status. Since status is positioned in a group, a person has as many statuses as he has group affiliations. For instance, one might have the status of a male, an adult, a husband and a father.

He also has status in his occupational group as well as other groups that he is a part of. Some of his statuses are based on biological factors, for example, his sex and age and others on the basis of merit. For example, being a husband, we refer to the first type of status as an ascribed status and to the second one as an achieved status. An ascribed status is assigned at birth on the basis of biological factors. The most common ones are sex, race and age. The achieved status is the status one has earned to further understand them.

Let's examine how society regulates the status of individuals. According to age, an individual's privileges and obligations change as he grows older. In our society, for example, a very young child enjoys certain immunities. He is held to be incapable of crime, hence cannot be punished by the law. On the other hand, he is subject to special restrictions. He must go to school. He cannot marry. He cannot vote.

The fact that he is a child plays an important part in defining his role in the group. The specific respects in which children's roles differ from those of adults in each group vary from culture to culture. But such differences exist everywhere. All in all, people are given various statuses. These statuses determine the roles they must play in the group. This assorting process is called social differentiation and goes on in all societies. For example, women have a status distinct from that of men, and children have a status unlike that of adults.

Why is society interested in assigning an immediate status to the individual? Usually this is the case because the earlier people are adjusted to a particular status, the more efficiently they are likely to function. And additionally, everyday business of society cannot be left to chance. Let's review the key points of this chapter. Our social status represents our position in a group. Depending on our status, we are assigned a role. In other words, we are expected to perform certain functions.

We have as many statuses as we have group affiliations. We might be given a status by birth. This is referred to as a scribe status or we might earn it. This is called achieving status. The process of giving a status and subsequent roles to us is what we call social differentiation. This process is necessary for the efficient execution of our functions in a group.

What Is Social Class?

Social class. Our status is our position in a group, particularly significant as a determinant of status is our social class. In this chapter, we will learn what a social class is, how it is determined and the hierarchy between classes. We will also learn about social mobility. A social class is the aggregate of persons having essentially the same social status in a given society. These people enjoy the same level of respect and have the same level of assumed competence in that society.

How is our social class determined? Usually in today's day and age, in most societies, people are grouped together based on socioeconomic factors like wealth, income, education, occupation, race and gender, among others. For instance, to identify one social class, we can examine the clubs to which he belongs, the size of his fortune and the circles in which he moves. When considering his social class we pass over his status in individual groups and we focus on his status in the social set.

For example, he might have a great reputation as a scientist, but that doesn't mean that he is part of the upper class for reasons such as poverty or race. Thus, class status overshadows all other statuses. How are societies with social classes structured? Not all societies are composed of social classes, but those that do, have a social structure that generally resembles a pyramid. The lowest social class is at the base of the pyramid and the other social classes are arranged above it in a hierarchy of rank and distinction.

This grouping of people based on social classes is what is referred to as social stratification. Since there is a hierarchy of rank, the fundamental characteristic of a social class is its position of relative superiority or inferiority to other social classes. Why would a class be superior to another? This is because those in the higher social classes receive better social rewards. They are more socially acceptable and they have a high standard of living. Thus, it doesn't come as a surprise that most of us would prefer to be identified with the upper class.

But does that guarantee that we would receive those same rewards more often than not? That is very likely. Typically, the members of the same class have more or less the same life chances. They have the same probability of securing the good things of life, such as freedom, a high standard of living, leisure, deference or whatever things are highly valued in a given society. Thus, by belonging to the high class, we would get similar life chances with those in that class and we would also receive social rewards.

So for those of us that don't belong there already, is it possible to become a member of the upper class? Well, that depends. To answer this question, we need to look into the chances individuals have of changing their social class in a given society. This is what is referred to as social mobility. The good news is that in many societies it is not uncommon for individuals to move up or down the social ladder. Where this is the case, the society is said to have open classes. The bad news is that even in the most mobile of stratified societies, the great mass of individuals remain forever in the class into which they happen to be born. This can be shown, for example, by an examination of the statistics on occupations, marriage and the like for several generations of the population.

Sadly, the idea that opportunities are open equally to all individuals of equal ability must be regarded as a fantasy. So moving up the social ladder is very hard, but still possible in societies with open classes, social mobility is not allowed at all in societies with closed social classes. In these societies, individuals remain through a lifetime in the class into which they happen to be born. In other words, a class is strictly hereditary. Such closed classes are castes. In castes if your parents didn't belong to your desired caste, you would never be able, no matter what you did, to be part of it.

At the same time, your caste would determine not only the work you would do, the group within which you would marry, but the very routine of your daily conduct. Let's revisit the key points of this chapter. A social class is the aggregate of persons having essentially the same social status in a given society, our social class is determined predominantly by socioeconomic factors. Societies with social classes have a social structure that resembles a pyramid, signifying that there is a hierarchy between classes.

The superior classes offered to their members higher standards of living and more social rewards. Usually all the members of a class receive more or less the same rewards. The chances individuals have of moving up or down the social ladder is referred to as social mobility. Societies that allow social mobility have opened classes, whereas others that prohibit it have closed classes.

What Are The Differences Between Urban And Rural Communities?

Rural and urban. We rarely, if ever exist alone, we are linked in many different ways to a group. In infancy the most important group is our family. In later life, along with our family we become part of various groups. All these groups constitute a community in the particular area where we live. It is not surprising that we tend to resemble, in a sense, the community in which we live.

At the same time, people rarely rise much above the level of their community, thus choosing the right community to live in is important. In this chapter, we will learn about two large communities, the rural and the urban ones. We will compare the two and get an overview of the advantages and disadvantages of each. Before we analyze these two types of communities, we need to first note that there are several kinds of each.

For instance, in the United States, farmers generally live in a farmhouse located on the land they cultivate. Hence, the farming community is scattered over a large area and is sometimes referred to as the open country in contrast to the village. This mode of life differs from that in many parts of Europe, where the homes of the farmers are clustered in a village. Their lands often lie in narrow strips, some distance away from the village.

As you might expect, this difference, an ecological pattern, is accompanied by significant differences in social organization. European farmers, for example, are reputed to be more sociable, while American farmers are said to be more individualistic. Thus, European villagers and farming people are more cooperative. Their greater solidarity is basic to the greater influence which European farmers exert on European society.

Nonetheless, despite their differences, all rural communities have a few characteristics in common. They do not have many specialized stores, manufacturing establishments or different kinds of buildings for various purposes, as a result, usually small rural areas do not have specializations that enable each community to have a theater or, let's say, a store for furniture. Such lack of raise, no particular problem. But there is a serious social problem in other cases, such as the absence of libraries, high schools, hospitals which furnish needed social services to the people.

Recreational facilities are also limited in these rural communities. Why do rural communities lack these services? One major cause of these differences between rural and urban communities is the big difference in income. The cities have a greater per capita wealth than the rural communities. The multimillionaires are found in the cities. Even when the higher incomes in cities are accompanied by higher living costs and additional expenditures compared to those of rural communities, the range in prices and living costs is not as great as the range of incomes between villages and cities.

The economic prospects, as well as the opportunities for intellectual stimulation and amusement, contribute to the increased attractiveness for cities. But despite their advantages, we must keep in mind that cities are an artificial environment. The buildings are tall and crowded, close together so that the sky is less visible while the dust and smoke reduces the effectiveness of sunlight. Meanwhile, there is limited access to nature. Another characteristic of city life is living in close contact with such large numbers of people. This is accompanied by congestion and heterogeneity of the population, which in turn profoundly modify group life.

One of the biggest implications of large numbers living together is anonymity, a condition that is comparatively rare in small communities. In the latter, usually intimate primary group relationships prevail. In a large city different families living in the same apartment house may not be known to each other. These differences are significant. For instance, it is not easy in a small place for one person to steal from another, for he would have difficulty in using the stolen goods. The actions of an individual are more likely to be observed and gossip acts as a substitute for the police.

On the contrary, the conditions of city life are such as to favor stealing. This is the reason why it is said that crime is an urban phenomenon. Additionally, the contacts in cities are characterized by impersonality. The fact that it is easy to be lonely in a large city and not in a small town is of psychological significance. The closer identification with the group in a small place, though, lessening freedom of action may lead to more normal life for many individuals, especially for those who have been conditioned in early years to live in a close, small group.

Apart from loneliness, city residents are more likely to experience various mental health issues, such as depression, anxiety and schizophrenia compared to rural residents. Moreover, family life in the largest cities suffers by comparison with that of the smaller communities. The decline of the family is represented by fewer marriages, smaller families and less home ownership. As a result, there is a lower birth rate in urban areas compared to rural ones. Let's summarize what we learned in this chapter. There are various types of urban and rural communities with different social organizations. All the rural communities have in common that they lack some social services and recreational activities.

At the same time, they have lower income than urban communities. On the other hand, urban communities offer various economic prospects and opportunities for intellectual stimulation and amusement to their residents. But they lack access to nature. There is also congestion and heterogeneity of the population. As a result, there is more anonymity and impersonality. City residents are more likely to experience mental health issues. Meanwhile, family life also suffers in the largest cities.

How Is Society Organized?

Rural and urban. We rarely, if ever exist alone, we are linked in many different ways to a group. In infancy the most important group is our family. In later life, along with our family we become part of various groups. All these groups constitute a community in the particular area where we live. It is not surprising that we tend to resemble, in a sense, the community in which we live.

At the same time, people rarely rise much above the level of their community, thus choosing the right community to live in is important. In this chapter, we will learn about two large communities, the rural and the urban ones. We will compare the two and get an overview of the advantages and disadvantages of each. Before we analyze these two types of communities, we need to first note that there are several kinds of each.

For instance, in the United States, farmers generally live in a farmhouse located on the land they cultivate. Hence, the farming community is scattered over a large area and is sometimes referred to as the open country in contrast to the village. This mode of life differs from that in many parts of Europe, where the homes of the farmers are clustered in a village. Their lands often lie in narrow strips, some distance away from the village. As you might expect, this difference, an ecological pattern, is accompanied by significant differences in social organization.

European farmers, for example, are reputed to be more sociable, while American farmers are said to be more individualistic. Thus, European villagers and farming people are more cooperative. Their greater solidarity is basic to the greater influence which European farmers exert on European society. Nonetheless, despite their differences, all rural communities have a few characteristics in common. They do not have many specialized stores, manufacturing establishments or different kinds of buildings for various purposes, as a result, usually small rural areas do not have specializations that enable each community to have a theater or, let's say, a store for furniture. Such lack of raise, no particular problem.

But there is a serious social problem in other cases, such as the absence of libraries, high schools, hospitals which furnish needed social services to the people. Recreational facilities are also limited in these rural communities. Why do rural communities lack these services? One major cause of these differences between rural and urban communities is the big difference in income. The cities have a greater per capita wealth than the rural communities. The multimillionaires are found in the cities. Even when the higher incomes in cities are accompanied by higher living costs and additional expenditures compared to those of rural communities, the range in prices and living costs is not as great as the range of incomes between villages and cities.

The economic prospects, as well as the opportunities for intellectual stimulation and amusement, contribute to the increased attractiveness for cities. But despite their advantages, we must keep in mind that cities are an artificial environment. The buildings are tall and crowded, close together so that the sky is less visible while the dust and smoke reduces the effectiveness of sunlight. Meanwhile, there is limited access to nature. Another characteristic of city life is living in close contact with such large numbers of people. This is accompanied by congestion and heterogeneity of the population, which in turn profoundly modify group life.

One of the biggest implications of large numbers living together is anonymity, a condition that is comparatively rare in small communities. In the latter, usually intimate primary group relationships prevail. In a large city different families living in the same apartment house may not be known to each other. These differences are significant. For instance, it is not easy in a small place for one person to steal from another, for he would have difficulty in using the stolen goods.

The actions of an individual are more likely to be observed and gossip acts as a substitute for the police. On the contrary, the conditions of city life are such as to favor stealing. This is the reason why it is said that crime is an urban phenomenon. Additionally, the contacts in cities are characterized by impersonality. The fact that it is easy to be lonely in a large city and not in a small town is of psychological significance. The closer identification with the group in a small place, though, lessening freedom of action may lead to more normal life for many individuals, especially for those who have been conditioned in early years to live in a close, small group.

Apart from loneliness, city residents are more likely to experience various mental health issues, such as depression, anxiety and schizophrenia compared to rural residents. Moreover, family life in the largest cities suffers by comparison with that of the smaller communities. The decline of the family is represented by fewer marriages, smaller families and less home ownership. As a result, there is a lower birth rate in urban areas compared to rural ones. Let's summarize what we learned in this chapter.

There are various types of urban and rural communities with different social organizations. All the rural communities have in common that they lack some social services and recreational activities. At the same time, they have lower income than urban communities. On the other hand, urban communities offer various economic prospects and opportunities for intellectual stimulation and amusement to their residents. But they lack access to nature.

There is also congestion and heterogeneity of the population. As a result, there is more anonymity and impersonality. City residents are more likely to experience mental health issues. Meanwhile, family life also suffers in the largest cities.

What Are The Origins Of Our Economic Institutions?

Economic institutions. There is a close connection between economics and culture. The economic processes concerning exchange, trade, production and distribution are very much in accord with the values of the community. In this chapter, we will learn about the origins of our economic life in order to get a comprehensive picture of the development of our current economic organization.

Our present elaborate economic organization had its humble origins in the food gathering cultures hundreds of thousands of years ago. The earliest economic activities consisted largely in searching for fruits, nuts, grains and grains and hunting of animals among primitive people. There is no separate economic organization such as we have today, but a beginning is found in the division of labor between men and women. Men are generally hunters.

Women are more often the gatherers of plants and seeds. Primitive people do not generally live in single families, but in small communities or bands of a score of individuals or a score or more of families. Thus, the hunting and gathering might be supplemented by the community. These communities are self-sufficient. In other words, they produce everything they need and as a result, there is no need to trade items. Therefore, trading does not appear to be instinctive or even natural. It has to be invented or learned.

And apparently it is a late social invention in the evolution of culture. Within the community the main mechanisms of exchange are hospitality and gifts. Services are rendered or goods given without payment, but with the expectation of a later return in kind. It is interesting to note that the hunting people remember with great precision the value of the gift, there are no wages, but the general understanding about labor is that if you help me, I will help you some time to exactly the same degree.

When it comes to property, there is private ownership of personal items such as clothing, weapons and tools, but they collectively share the land and the food supply. These goods were relatively scarce. Primitives generally strived not so much for private gain as for status and reputation. The best hunter not only has the most food, he also has the biggest reputation. Eventually, they discovered how to domesticate animals, particularly the big animals such as cattle and how to cultivate plants. In other words agriculture. The development of agriculture and of the parallel pastoral economy meant a more certain and substantial food supply and a larger population.

With a stable life of agriculture, there seemed to have been associated other inventions, such as pottery making and weaving. Pursuits as such require advanced skills and out of 100 individuals, some would do a job better than others. These are the ones likely to specialize. The foundations of exchange were thus laid. Under agriculture there was a greater chance of trade. In time pastoral life and agriculture were brought together in farm life. By now, property had become highly developed.

Since agriculture emphasized the private ownership of land, there was also individual ownership of equipment and products. This, in return resulted in a growth of property in the competition between our quest for possessions and our desire for intangible values such as reputation or affection. The former was gaining ground during this period. The handicrafts flowered, enriching the material culture, further increasing the social emphasis on the acquisition of material objects.

The greater the variety and number of such objects of hand manufacture, the greater the requirement of labor. And hence there was an impetus to an extension of the division of labor beyond the principles of sex and age. Specialization was furthered by the discoveries of the use of copper, tin, gold, bronze and iron. Since it was not easy for each household or each male in a houschold to become adept in the working of metals, the development of specialists outside each family meant that there had to be a further exchange of goods. With specialization in the handicrafts and improvements in transportation the volume of trade increased.

One evidence of this was the city which may be thought of as a place where the inhabitants do not grow enough food to feed themselves. They therefore must import it from outside, which means transportation and trade and exchange cloth, leather, metal goods or something else for it. Trade was predominantly by barter. There were some goods and frequent demand which were exchanged most often when such goods were light and durable, as was the case with gold and silver ornaments, money developed.

Let's summarize what we learned in this chapter, our economic organization has its origins in the food gathering cultures that existed hundreds of thousands of years ago.

Primitive people used to gather plants and animals. There was a division of labor in these activities. They lived in self-sufficient communities where they exchanged services and gifts when it came to property. They had a few personal items, but they shared the land and the food supply.

Things changed when they discovered how to domesticate animals and developed agriculture. The ownership of land was emphasized at the same time the stable access to food allowed for more inventions to exercise the new skills related to them. One had to develop some expertise. Therefore, specialization of labor emerged. At the same time, they had to exchange the goods that they produced for other goods. Thus, the need for trade arose later, with further specialization and improvements in transportation, trading was increasing and money was developed. All these advances greatly speeded the development of some of the economic processes familiar to us.

How Was Capitalism Developed & What Are Its Implications?

Capitalism. In this chapter, we will continue exploring how the economic organization has evolved throughout the years to our present day. We will also discuss some of the shortcomings of our modern economic system of capitalism and how they are being ameliorated preceding the emergence of our modern order. The necessity for protection against marauding groups in Europe led to the feudal type of organization, especially where a central government did not exist or was breaking up. Owners of property and large holders of land found they could extract payments of money or goods from weaker farmers.

With this money, soldiers could be maintained with their soldiers. They secured control over surrounding neighbors and offered protection to the farmers. Gradually, wealth started to accumulate in the hands of a few. This led to greater division of labor and to an increase in the variety of goods produced. During this period a great step forward was taken with the development of power beyond that supplied by human beings and domesticated animals, especially the development of steam in making steel tools.

Steam power gave a great impetus to production as the volume and variety of economic goods increased and the differentiation between consumers, goods and producer goods became more pronounced. Producer goods were now more intricate, expensive and more difficult to acquire because financing was necessary. Money for their purchase was called capital, and the raw materials and tools purchased were known as capital goods. Sometimes the heads of two or more families joined forces to conduct the business better or to increase their capital.

A drawback to this practice was that each partner in such an economic organization was liable for the whole indebtedness of the partnership, which was a protection for the creditors. At the same time, such a partnership was not always available to meet the expanding needs of business. Thus began a movement away from family domination of industry. The availability of funds was a service better furnished by the corporation, which made it possible for any number of persons to supply the needed capital. In return, each investor received his proportionate share of stock and was in general liable only up to the value of the shares he held.

When the corporation was very large, the ownership was divorced from management. Management was then delegated to a committee who chose a president or manager. So different was this new type of industrial life from that of the household economy and the handicrafts that a special name was devised for it. Because Capital played such a prominent part in financing the new system, it was called capitalism. In particular capitalism is a large system which includes production, transportation and distribution, which employs labor, pays interest and dividends on investments and supplies the great variety of wants of large, heterogeneous populations.

This type of economic organization has been the prevailing one in the expansion and growth of industry in the Western world. It has raised the standard of living and built a marvelous economic civilization. Despite its benefits it also has a few disadvantages. Firstly, the shareholders and the management of the corporation are removed from intimate contact with the workers, a situation which results in impersonal and unsatisfactory labor relations. Secondly, there is also much difficulty in providing regular employment.

The smooth operation of our complex economic system depends on the synchronization of many parts. A common factor of turmoil is business depression, which often leads to increase in unemployment. The large-scale introduction of automation that reduces the need for labor also creates considerable unemployment, at least temporarily. Additionally, there is a marked inequality in the distribution of the wealth produced under private capitalism. Not everyone gets the same income.

The salary of a rich person is multiple times as much as the poor person. These are only wages. The rich person also received interest on bonds and dividends on stock so that the variation in income is even greater. Furthermore, sometimes businesses try to eliminate the competition and maximize profits by creating monopolies. This happens because in some types of business, a tremendous initial capital is required to start it. Therefore, less people can afford it.

Consequently, there is no competition to keep the prices of the products these businesses produce down. Since one business controls the supply, it can also control the price. Usually a private, unregulated monopoly maintains the price which will give it the greatest total profit. In some cases, when only a few owners of a particular business remain they often get together and agree on a price that will give each one a profit. To protect both workers and the public against exploitation the government undertakes to regulate some businesses and to aid other businesses.

Usually, the state regulates monopolies to allow for healthy competition. It creates minimum wage laws designed to raise the incomes at the lower classes and to combat the inequalities in income. It sets up income taxes that take a larger proportion of high incomes. Let's revisit the key points of this chapter. Feudalism is the economic system where owners of large property receive payments from farmers in exchange for protection. This led to the accumulation of wealth in the hands of a few to increased specialization and to an increased variety of goods.

Eventually, the machinery that was used to produce consumer goods became intricate and expensive. Thus families had to combine their capital to afford it. Since this wasn't always an option, corporations offered the necessary funds with the help of shareholders. Eventually, the corporation dominated the industry and it gave rise to our current economic system of capitalism. Capitalism raises the standard of living, but it has some shortcomings. These include impersonal labor, unemployment, inequality in wealth distribution and rise of monopolies. To counteract these problems, governments take measures by passing laws to protect workers, consumers and other businesses.

What Constitutes A Family And How Was It Developed?

Family origins. Our home is the place where our personal and social virtues are developed, the type of citizen we become is related closely to the type of mother, father and home life we have. In this chapter, we will study the family in the earliest hunting cultures and what changes occurred in it as the material culture developed into our present civilization.

By doing so, we will get a better understanding of our family life today and its possible changes in the future. When you picture a family, what comes to mind? Most people would picture an association of husband and wife with or without children, or of a single parent, man or woman with children. In other words, the mates and their offspring, the mates have distinctive sex and functions that constitute the primary reason for the creation of the institution. This type of family is referred to as the nuclear family.

Others, when picturing a family, would include a part from the parents and their children. More individuals such as grandparents, relatives, in-laws and grandchildren. This larger family forms a unit which we call a household. Therefore, it is significant that the structure of the family is not fixed. It varies in different cultures. Likewise, the functions of the family are flexible.

The family may do few or many things. For instance, the family may provide economic services for its members. It may help to educate them, give them religious guidance, furnish recreation, protect them against dangers of various sorts, and provide affection and connection. The family that consists of a male one or more females and children with perhaps a relative or so is found in every hunting society known to us. No matter how simple its culture, the husband is a hunter.

The wife prepares food and the women and children help to gather wild vegetables, to dig roots or to pick berries. Besides getting food and caring for the young, the anthropoids help each other in fights and the male protects the female against marauding males. The early family group seems to have many resemblances to the modern family in its small size and limited economic and social functions. Thus, the history of the family does not suggest any great evolution.

Nonetheless, the family has varied greatly in different cultures. Such variations are evident when we look into the institution of marriage. Most marriages all over the world, even among preliterate people, consist of one husband and one wife. That is to say, monogamy is practiced more largely than any other arrangement. But we also encounter cultures where polygamy, the marriage of more than one female to one male or polyandry, the marriage of more than one female to one male are favored.

Additionally, the family has shown a great deal of variation at different time periods. Our modern family stands in marked contrast to the earlier agricultural family. In the latter, economic functions are particularly prominent, the family being an almost completely self-sustaining business enterprise.

In particular, with the advent of the plough and the domestication of cattle, the various handicrafts became much more highly developed. Such things as the grinding of grain, preparation of soap molding of pottery, fabrication of leather, construction of furniture and concoction of medicines were done at the homestead by members of the household.

Thus, while developing a variety of important economic activities, the household had become a significant business enterprise. Under these conditions, marriage was favored since a wife was needed on the farm and children were useful workers. In such a system, the efficiency and suitability of mates was emphasized over affection as a basis for marriage. A man usually looked for a good housekeeper and a woman for a capable provider. A good marriage was thought to be one in which the capabilities of the young couple were high, rather than one where the love element was strong.

While love was regarded as a desirable factor for marriage, it was not important enough to be the sole basis for it. It was assumed that after marriage, affection and congeniality would develop between the couple, the system gave rise to a highly developed household economy, which existed in Europe through the Middle Ages into the nineteenth century. The same type of family is also found widely distributed in Asia. This household economy was developed chiefly in villages around which agriculture was practiced or in the open country where farms were scattered for only a very small percentage of the population lived in cities.

Let's summarize what we learned in this chapter: our families shape our personality, their various types of families, but the most common today is the nuclear family. The structure of the family has varied across cultures and time periods, but it is always based around the mates and their offspring. The families between primitive people were small and had limited economic function. Extended economic function had the agricultural families where the members of the family exercised important economic activities within it. As a result, creating a family was a necessity. During that time, less emphasis was placed on affection and love between the couples, but rather on their capacities to work efficiently.

What Are The Characteristics Of Modern Families?

Modern families. With the growth of the factory system and the rise of cities, family life undergoes profound changes. In this chapter we will explore the effects of these changes in the structure of the family as well as the characteristics of our modern family. One change that had a significant impact on the evolution of the family was the transfer of the production from the home to the factory with the development of various inventions, such as the use of steam as a source of power applied to tools and with the availability of cheaper iron and steel, big machinery was developed.

This type of machinery required more space and more workers than were to be found in the household. The need for labor in various handicrafts was not so much for family labor as for individual labor. Eventually, the factory, instead of the homestead, became the unit of production. The process of the transfer of economic functions from the urban family to outside agencies has gone quite far in the past century. Only activities such as cooking the care of the house and laundering are left now chiefly in the urban family.

But even promotions of the latter functions have been transferred as, for instance, cooking of lunches to restaurants and some laundering to outside laundries. The transfer process is not yet finished. Men's functions were among the first to leave the homestead as farming was given up. Women's more varied household duties have been transferred more slowly.

This decline in the economic significance of the family led to its transformation to the type of family most of us are familiar with today.

One of its typical characteristics is its small size. The family is now shaped more closely than ever before around the marital pair. This is the case because the economic activities of the family no longer require the assistance of relatives and married children. Hence, there is no longer any need for their presence in the household. Moreover, the natural biological family itself is contracting in size. Children are expensive to have. So with the advancement in the knowledge and methods of contraception, having children depends on the discretion of the couple.

At the same time, it isn't as necessary as before to create a family. A mate is no longer automatically a worker and an economic asset as before, but may now be an economic liability. Hence the economic motives for marriage, long characteristic of the institution, ceased to be prominent. As a result in urban communities, the proportion of individuals not living in any family is large. For instance, in the United States, single person households have doubled over the last fifty years.

In Norway and Sweden, they are half of the total number of households with the economic function of the family diminished. What prompts us to form families? Nowadays, increasing emphasis is placed on psychological values such as affection, companionship and emotional security. Many families have as their main function that of providing affection between the mates. In the light of the foregoing, it is to be expected that in marriage today, the affectional element would be emphasized to the extreme.

The present emphasis on affection as the chief basis for marriage means that companionship is the principal benefit sought from the union. The main concern of mates with each other is one of happiness. At the same time, the family system is necessary for the rearing of young children. The very early years of a child's life are spent almost exclusively in the family. Thus, since the personality of the child is dependent upon the way the early years are spent, the responsibility placed on the parents seems to be very great. Even when the children are of school age, the parents still educate their children. At the same time, parents strive to provide a happy and wholesome childhood for their young.

The changes in incentives for formation of the family influence the strength of the tie uniting the couple, formerly the family, was held together by many different bonds, economic and religious. At present, the chief remaining bond is affection. One bond does not hold as firmly as several. The affectional bond is often very strong at the inception of marriage, but it does not always endure. When it breaks, married couples naturally wish to separate from each other. About 45 percent of married couples in the United States divorce.

Yet ordinary observation suggests that all disappointed couples do not resort to such drastic action. Some remain together despite their difficulty. There are a few factors that contribute to this. Usually, couples that have been married for many years are less likely to separate. In the United States sixty percent of all divorces involve individuals aged 25 to 39, at the same time, married couples are held together by children. In the United States. About 65 percent of divorces are granted to childless couples. Thus, affection and responsibility for children tend to hold the family together.

Another factor affecting the stability of marriage is the type of community in which the family lives. For instance, in cities, the divorce rate is much higher than in rural regions. Finally, religion is a factor that influences the stability of the family. Some religions permit separation, but not divorce, forbidding a second marriage. Other churches deplore the breaking of the marriage time, but condone it under a variety of circumstances. Let's review what we discussed in this chapter.

The different functions of the family found in the various preliterate cultures and in the historical periods shows that the family has changed a good deal in the past and has assumed many different forms and functions. The family has proved to be a very resilient and flexible institution, despite radical changes in form and function. The family has continued to exist in every society known to us. The craving for affection and the need of rearing children have undoubtedly been fundamental factors in making the family an omnipresent and enduring social institution.

What has been happening in recent years is the decline of the family as an economic institution. So great has been the change that today we think of the family chiefly as an institution for the provision of marital happiness and the rearing of children.

What Are The Origins Of Government & Which Are Its Functions?

Government. Every day of our lives, we come in contact directly or indirectly with the government. State policies affect the price and amount of food, clothing and fuel we buy. They also regulate our recreational activities and tell us what we can and cannot do. A fair sized proportion of all the money we earn must be paid to the government in taxes in many countries.

The government provides medical care for us when we are sick and gives us aid when we are out of work. These are only a few examples of how the government affects our lives. Since the government plays such an important role, it is necessary to take a look backward at its origins and to see something of how it has varied in time. We will also discuss what functions the government undertakes, as well as the types of government placing special emphasis on democracies. What is the government? It is an organization which maintains order for the whole group. Such an organization is lacking among primitive people with the simplest material culture. They have no specially constituted government.

This is evident from the fact that they have no established rulers. But when a special occasion arises which calls for group action, a temporary leader may be selected. His leadership ceases, when the work is done. The lack of government can be attributed to the fact that there is a little disorder among them. Disorders which do occur are handled by organizations such as the family and the clan. The groups are very small, which means that public opinion can operate effectively as a regulatory force. The idea of government as a special separate institution gains in favor as the conception of the group as a whole entity develops.

When families are organized along kinship lines into clans, there is a sense of locality. Thus, those settlements which are contiguous, have a consciousness of belonging to the same kind. This unity sets them apart from outsiders. Consequently, local bands become affiliated in sentiment forming tribes. The tribe may be regarded as the forerunner of the state. Since tribes develop under a plethora of factors in different places, there is not a uniform development of government for all cultures. Hence, it is not possible to trace the evolution of the state except for particular groups.

What may be shown, however, are the principal factors which are correlated with the development of government. A crisis involving the whole group or territory is the sort of situation out of which the idea of discipline for the whole group would arise. Serious competition between whole groups would also seem to be favorable to the creation of the state. This competition might even lead to war, which requires organized force between two politically independent units in pursuit of tribal policy.

Other factors are the presence of dominant personalities, conquest and social classes. When we have some or multiple of these factors interrelated, a state is formed. Different combinations of these factors produce different types of government in various societies. Fast forward in modern times, states are everywhere and the scope of the state has expanded enormously. Some of its functions usually have been the promotion of general welfare, administration of justice, national defense, as well as economic and social regulation. Governments render these services and exert the controls through national and local agencies of many different types. Some are democratic and others dictatorial.

In other words, in some countries the government's purpose is to serve the individual, and in others the individual is said to exist for the good of the state. Since the mid 1970s, there has been an upward trend toward democracies around the world. The adoption of democracy has been encouraged by a wider education and a higher standard of living. The masses, because of public education and higher wages, are more capable of voting intelligently and are able to contribute more taxes. One of the most important benefits of democracy is the power of the people is available as a check against abuses by elected officials.

But in cases where the people are not fully oriented and interested, it is in those who thus circumvent the people. Such groups are party cliques and special pressure groups. In most cases, their goal is to get the government to do something for them. Let's review what we learned in this chapter. Indirectly or directly, we always come in contact with the government. Such an organization is lacking among primitive people. With the conception of the group as a whole entity the idea of government emerges. Even though the evolution of the state cannot well be traced, it is possible to indicate factors and situations correlated with the conception of the state.

Such factors are crisis, competition and conquest. Governmental institutions today are mostly focused on promoting general welfare, and most of them are democratic. Despite the fact that the power in a democracy lies within the people it is not uncommon to witness corruption.

Cyber Security From Beginner to Expert

This Book is an actionable, step-by-step beginner's guide to locking hackers, identity thieves, and cyber criminals out of your life once and for all.

Today's reality is yesterday's science fiction.

You can have a real-time video conversation with someone on the other side of the planet, you can send and receive money without even taking out your wallet, and you can post content online that reaches millions of people in a matter of minutes.

Unfortunately, the same technology that enables all this new freedom and convenience also exposes us to new security threats that we've never encountered.

Malware that infects your computer and watches everything you do, phishing scams that steal private information from millions of people—today's digital world is a criminal's playground. It makes the process of stealing money or even stealing someone's entire identity way more efficient.

The worst part? You are a target.

Many people neglect taking steps to protect themselves online because they think, "Why would anyone want to steal my information?"

Well, for starters, if you have any money to your name at all, there are plenty of tech-savvy criminals out there who are patiently waiting for the opportunity to take it from you.

Beyond that, they can also steal your identity to run up charges on your credit cards, open new utility accounts, get medical treatment using your health insurance, or take advantage of your friends and family by impersonating you on social media.

Again, this is a beginner-level Book. These are technical topics, but I hope to walk you through everything in a way that's actionable and easy to understand.

If you haven't already, be sure to enroll in the Book! I can't wait to see you inside.

Understanding The Cyber Security Role Using A Sample Job Description

We want to look at the first day the stock, and then we can move to the other one, basic information, the security program manager role, it involves a lot of engineering as well. I believe it's an output of one of the or rather all of the security information systems itself. Right. I mean, all the domains would probably be covering operations, part of it, etc. Yeah, I just briefly went to but again, so I thought, I'll go through this one with you, focus on the job first and kind of you don't really understand what the expectations are here. Right. So, so, so it says OK, this is what the recruiter sent me. Right.

What, whatever notes are observations are. So I'm just forwarded whatever she sent me to you guys. So what's it all about? Those poll numbers, collaboration, the partnership idea to select the integral managed services for veterans groups. That one important role involves risk misuse, case study deadlines coming across to start detection, logic, Patronus security audit management. Yeah, this is the second biggest piece here.

I just think that people management skills and all that, that's not a concern at this point of time because obviously as we continue we'll be solving the technical part of it, which is the main concern, you know. Exactly, exactly. Within it you'll develop that part. But it was unknown. One, the pictures and closed society. That's one of the things you do find the risk.

The best use is to use GIs, target and cross tools. Yeah, but there is a basic U.S. target landscape and cross to stack the picture like this has been highlighted twice. And I also told myself that this is what I also need to focus a lot about from the other use case scenario that we will be discussing in the interview. So this has been informed to me that this would be the primary point of discussion at some point of time toward the interviews here. Yeah. Yeah, they can talk about how so-called recovery continues and the risk management reporting project related to activities takes equity.

Also, this is one. What we offer, should you apply? Finding the ship and then getting the functionality of stock into the response that this is one. Must have been a hands on experience in dealing operating. Yeah, that's too strong a clear track record, extended lessons, but previous exposure to it. The experience, integrity, automation and programming by 10. They might look at this knowledge of Christian science and see that response best practices probably will look at this. Mr. Samay says that that's one of the very high discussion points that they will bring across. And also the meteor attack is what they were talking about this morning.

I actually have to go through a small discussion with the recruiter. And she told me that if you look at the operations role, I mean, in the same company for the manager, the stock manager who is comfortable performing right now, she got somewhat in touch with a guy to speak to him, asking what would be your general rule and responsibilities. He did mention that, you know, all of this automation of the job description is part of it, obviously, but also they would be focusing more on the attack and all mortar attacks and also lots and lots of scenario based questions would be coming across in terms of how the logs would be generated and how would you start giving different answers in terms of recording the logs and etc..

That is one and second is a different kind of instance on these issues that would have happened previously in any organization, different incidents and how the resolution should be in productiveness. What kind of scenario happens and how could you probably answer? These are sort of things that were just part of a highlight to the recruiter at this point. Yeah, OK, let me. Yeah, so, OK, let's go through this first. So when they say that you have to be, you know, SELEK, develop and implement security solutions, that's obviously will be part of, you know, managing us all our broader information security. Right. So are you OK?

The way I want to present that is so there are things like I'm going to use a mind map for that and you have your parameters. Then you have your cloud, the new perimeter, right, then your end point, then your servers, then your databases. So when we need to understand what other layers, you know, what the security layers have been, what's in place like, you know, what am I supposed to protect? The one first thing is you'll say, OK, what the perimeter looks like, not the very outer layer of the protection.

Which is what is my edge of those edge gateways, edge firewalls. So then you have to get OK, what are my safe parameters to be your firewalls and you know, OK, so security, you just want to know what inventory would be part of the so-called perimeter. I don't know if I was one of them, but is there any other component from this MTV that would be part of the perimeter acknowledgment perimeter would be your ideas about intrusion prevention detection systems, which would be on the perimeter? Because what happens is the way you deploy your firewalls. Right. And then you'll have your ideas. Ideas. OK. Right, because you have your seat. That's why I'm saying, you know, this is your outer ring, which is the perimeter of your organization. Right.

And then you have your if this is the perimeter, look, virtually the right guy comes in and hits your perimeter, which is the firewall, which is which is allowing the inbound traffic to your organization. But it looks at it and it says, OK, you know what, my security organization has set some rules or firewall design policies which will drop the traffic. So 80 percent of the traffic gets dropped at your perimeter firewall. Right. Right. So then what you do is you put your other protection intrusion prevention system at the perimeter, which even further reduces your incoming traffic.

And the attack, you might ask, like, you know, OK, what type of graphics do you think will come? An example. I'm just imagining you have a Web server hosted, for example, a company. So obviously the Port Hedland port for three will be open. The traffic, the firewall will allow the traffic to come through. But what if the traffic in Port 1840 is malicious? How do you detect that? And that's where your idea comes into the picture, right? The ideas, that type of traffic and I love you only traffic, which is more or less it feeds itself. Right. And then it kind of allows you and then the internal internal network is there where we call the DMZ zone. Right.

So it's like the buffer between your external and internal network. So, you know, it's like, how do I say that? It gets us. But I think a buffer zone where you can go in, but you can't come out the same way. Correct. So you have your parameter Yagur DMZ, then you have your internal network and then your conduit, either it can be a security application, security, or other data security. So it would be the perimeter. I understand that and then you would definitely have your DMZ. If you're coming from a financial market, say definitely a bit of a DMZ because you need external parties to come in with your product or service or whatever it is, then you would have your DMZ. Other security, internal security. That's what you're telling me?

Yeah, exactly, something like this. So you have your firewalls here, the ones the traffic hits your firewall, it gets filtered out. It comes in your ideas, ideas. If the traffic again, right. When it comes to your authentication, how do you then you'll have to to get to a system to gain access. Right. Either to credential order or a token or whatever the authentication mechanisms. Once you get authentication, then your system will address you and then you'll get access to a system, whatever that is. And this is just an access model. But if you see this so if you see this, that's what you're paying me. You know how this is for you to get a higher level understanding of how you perceive protecting or how you perceive creating a use case or a right talking about it. So what do I do?

I when you're talking about what is it you're going to do? The first thing is to understand what my opinion is. What are my layers of protection? And for each layer, what type of protection do I have? Like what type of protection do I have for Internet security? DMZ, who can access DMZ where the DMZ access can be filtered from which firewalls, which devices are allowed to connect to DMZ?

What is closer to the DMZ? Either it's a web application, you exchange your databases, whatever that is. Right. Which is close to the DMZ, what it looks like for me and what is exposed to the perimeter and DMZ, that means what is exposed to your Internet. How much of that is my exposure to it? And then you'll come back and then I look at my DMZ, you say, OK, what is my DMZ? Then I look at my internal network.

What are my internal network ranges? What is the composition of my Internet? Do I have an internal firewall which can access as the final output from the internal network output to the DMZ or do the right then I understand like you know, but they understand the internal network where they are located, where the topology of it is. What components are there are networks which are out there, a firewall which is in which does that. Because sometimes what happens is.

On the perimeter, you have a firewall, which could be, for example, a juniper firewall, right. So which could allow you the traffic to come in and hit your DMV with all your applications right. Right. So now what you do is, OK, you have a firewall which allows the traffic to come and hit your web applications, which are posted on the Internet for the public to access. But you have a different firewall for the users to go to. So they will not use the Juniper firewall, but they use up all the firewalls to go to the Internet. So you are distinguishing them from the traffic.

You're segregating the traffic. OK, the user traffic control network will go through a different road and the traffic will come through a different firewall. So there is no link between data leakage or no connection between these two traffic. So that's what you need to understand on the Internet. What I have offered to get fired. Well, then a little bit different use cases for that, right? I have a different use. Cases are different monitoring levels for.

Right, because the rules have been used to be very strict and what does it take to protect, you know, and do I have an idea as perimeter to kind of a lot more traffic? No obligation or not? Again, a big question. Right, then, once you understand these layers, once you understand, OK, what were perimeter watches, my physical security looks like, what my internal traffic is, what my whole security is, what my application security is, and where is my data residing? What are my databases? What's my storage?

Looks like a backup and everything else looks like right now. So I'm going to look at this and let me give you this. Chad. Yeah, so that's how you have to look at this, you know, first things first, a conceptual way you have to understand, like how it's architecture, like what my looks like because I understand what you imagine your house, your own, you have your own individual house. What's your biggest risk? What's the biggest risk that you'll face? Right. It's your bedroom, your main gate and your main door are the only things which are protecting you. Right.

And if you have an eye on them, like who's going and who's coming in on the perimeter, you know, if you can allow based on either the facial detection or by an accessory guard who should come in and who should go out. Right. So if you understand your perimeter, you'll understand what you're exposing yourself to. Right. You don't want it right on your wall. What's the exact address, your full name, your full phone number. Right.

You just want to be as discreet as possible. Like a post-box number. That's pretty much it. You don't want anything else. But if somebody is trying to give out a full nameplate and that's calling for more trouble, no. So that you'll understand what's your exposure from a perimeter point of view, what you're exposing to what the attacker can see. And that's what you want to see as well. Right. So one good thing, what you can do is you can use something called as there is a site called Shodan, which is basically, uh, uh, an Internet scanner. Right.

So let's take an example of abuse, IPTV. So this site, again, you know, just an example. The sites are more or less for repetition, so we use a busybody to check for a repetition of an IP address. Right. I'm just showing an example. So, you know, this is your company's IP address example. So you want to see that? OK, I want to know what my exposure is. You know, what does the Internet see when I type an IP address for my company? I see this, so it means there is a port authority which is open and it's running an index and over and this is the whole information. OK, what can I deal with?

I know there is a port city open, but is there anything else which is open on that IP address. Right. So an example could be HDFC. Bank dot com. I'm just typing something. So now you see, what type of information does it give you? It basically gives you, says IBM, its GDP. So now you're curious. You know what? What does this IBM, you go back and open and you said, oh, isn't that a site which is open, which is the DOT EFC? So now you know that there is something out there which is showing something in some information for my company.

Right from a perimeter point of view. Right, sometimes it can also show that there is a firewall which is open to the firewall login, which is open to the Internet or the domain, the company website itself is showing up here with a lot of other details. It can show you a lot of other details, like, OK, I've got an IBM HTTP server. There is some extreme option which is enabled here, the back of the name of the IP address and everything else which is out there. Right.

So just to understand what your exposure levels are, you can use this like what are you using for the exposure level? What are we looking at? We're looking at a Web site that shows that is it or is it just a short shot under the Internet scanner, scans the entire Internet and lets me know what is exposed for that company. OK, so I can just as an example, give me a company name, one of your friends, company name or any company name which you think you want to take here. You could take Maybank in just about any way. Bank dot com.

OK, OK, well, let me get it. Our conduct is just as good as mine then, but not mine. We've got com dot. Is he right? Yes. So now you are basically. There is a login page. What does this mean? So it's showing me eating my bank dot, dot com, dot, right? And if it's providing me something which is not supposed to be exposed, this is a risk for you, right? So use of the system is the secret, you know, but that's all there. But whatever we see here is actually in the DMZ. That's what you mean to say? It's not exactly. But, you know, probably the DMZ could be hosted on the Internet, but accidentally exposed. All right.

I'm just looking at exposed levels of a company or what is exposed for a company, right? What it exposes for a company. So when you understand what is exposed to a company, you become much larger now. So you understand what your exposure level now you're going to go back and say that, OK, you know what? Where is this application, whether it's on the DMCA ordered on the Internet host, what is the risk based approach now? If somebody can get onto the site, what can happen to my organization? Right. That's your risk based approach.

Well, if it's the DMCA and the policies, then the risk is very minimal. Right? If it's posted on the Internet or on the internal network and then you don't have proper rules in place to restrict the access, then your risk is way too high. What's the risk of doing so again, you know, so you can let's create a risk saying that, you know, side X post, because this is my, this is my side. What can happen here? Internal network. Then I say high risk. Right. Then it's a high risk y come on. Yeah. Escalation can happen. Propagation propagates. Propagation can happen. You can get a Propagator from that server to the server, right.

You know, they can compromise other Web servers, for example, I'm just saying. Yeah, yeah. Gain access to the server and from there they can do anything. So that's what you have to do is what are the risk exposure levels of what can happen from that and then try to understand what could be the impact for it, you know, where the attacker can jump from that particular system to other systems and what he can do. Right. So what goes on that system of how we connect to the other systems and then it can become too vulnerable because that can go anywhere from that. Exactly. Exactly. Exactly. That's the best approach is like, OK, what can happen? What's the risk for me? What what.

So I can understand the network there, you know, OK, this is a Web server connected to IT systems and that systems are connected with systems like you. You have to spread out a tree-like structure and try to understand, OK, what at the end what the attacker might look like and what the attacker will try to gain. You know, if he even gets to the tree, he'll get the credentials to almost all the systems in that environment. Right. Or if he if he leaves a malware on the server and tries to come back later in the year later, he's trying to do that in a way that you have understood that there is no exposure level there or how do I understand that the system is extremely clean, or do I have a prediction system prediction mechanism on the system to try to track the changes? Right.

And who are the users who are getting access to that? If the users get compromised, what will happen? Right. So that's how you'll have to think further and say that, OK, you know, what's my exposure level and what am I trying to do there? So that could be your initial perspective like, you know what, my let's watch my perimeter look like, what my internal holes are, what my exposure levels are, what are the current risks or what the company's facing? What have they done to protect their perimeter? Something like that, right, like an onion, you peel the layers layer by layer, so security is all about a layer by layer approach.

You can't just have one holistic approach. You know, you have to go layer by layer. So sure, I got to get to this physical security and the perimeter security will come to the physical in a bit. But Of course, physical is more about your cabling because I won't be talking about it. No, it's multiple things. So if in this case there is a whole concept of security. Right. It talks about your biometric access, your swipe cards, your biometric access, which is allowing your access to come in, who swipes in, who swipes out of the building, access to that as well. So imagine this.

You have a firewall which is super secure, which is super secure. You have climbed on the firewall so hard that nobody can come. But if you fail to secure your perimeter, which is your physical security, which is a building, then everything goes right because the building's security is because you're not protecting your physical assets. It means anybody can come in. Anybody can go. Yeah, right. So it can be that it can be accessing your physical infrastructure, which is your servers and switches and having the ability to plug in something like a rogue device operator.

You need to have that. So, you know, you don't you can't allow people to come in and, you know, access critical infrastructure or data centers. Right. So that's your physical security, so you have your camera systems, you have your Skype systems, how do you allow people to come in? Who are the people who have access to the systems? Usually I believe all of this is taking care of our data centers because most of the things are totally disconnected. Yeah, they definitely should. But again, you know, from our point of view, I can take care of physical security. Correct.

Like, if you're saying that there's a desktop on the office and somebody stole the desktop and it becomes an incident for us, it becomes an incident for security to take it, because the secret is where the physical security is also involved, but also in part because a system was stolen. Right. The first question is, if the system was stolen, what is the exposure for us, whether the thief he's selling the data to or selling the device to somebody else, can they access the data, which is on the server on that system and what they can do with that? Right. So then it becomes the whole picture of whether you have disk encryption enabled on that.

Do you have encryption enabled on that? Encryption enabled on that. So that's what Torquil will investigate. Was a user on that accessing that system, whether any suspicious login came from that user, even though a physical security breach. So I can see all of the things related to the user and the machine as well. Because, OK, what are you, what are you telling me is the worst case scenario is if let's say the physical asset is compromised, right? I mean, somebody steals the server. Let's just say for a minute, if they go into the cage, they take it out and they run away right now in that scenario. So the stock would have some kind of information where it would tell us that I can log in to that particular asset and tell you what resides on that particular site. Of course it can't.

Right, because it can tell you what kind of detail or what kind of web application to solicit and accept an application order. That is all fine. But apart from that. So wouldn't it be also responsible to get the stock to say that this is the kind of a protection that we have in place just in case expecting that somebody would steal the system? Exactly. That's what I said. The description is the first thing we ask what standard it has to be. So what happens is infosec decides as a policy, as a procedural standard that all the server should have encryption enabled. Right. So that no third party person can access the data.

Even they can have the disk in the position. They can't do anything about that I think. Right, right. Right. So that encryption standard has to be there, that this custom is encrypted first and then talk has to regularly monitor what is the system better, not whether this option is not enabled, either it's a new server or it's a new test of that. And then once we generate a report, the word exposes our team. You know, I think these are the servers which I see that they're newly come up and they don't have the description anywhere.

What do you want to do? Can you please go in? And this is as standard as the leader of the standard saying that this encryption has to be enabled. If they don't have that, if somebody has to monitor whether it's a server team or its assault team, the responsibility has to be there and monitor that and say that, OK, not because the biggest risk is for right. Because the information if the disk encryption is not enabled and stolen, it'll be an incident. And I can't do anything that I can do anything about. But after that, the fact that it's been stolen. Right. Then the second thing is.

And my point is, let's see if there are some of these standards that we have, these become part of the policy. I, like all the services, should be disk encrypted. And also they should be having the Salento version of antivirus installed on them. Just giving an example lined up right now. These all become part of a policy for the organization. Now, when these are not met physically, then they will start throwing letters and alerts to the SOC. Not because soccer is not part of the build process, officer.

All right, so I will not be part of the bills only when the server is in the production or it's put to use, then we can say that something was missing. But yeah, yeah, yeah, I get it. Point it should be, Of course, in the production, it should be the environment. And what my point is, but there has to be monitoring that sort of monitoring. Right. So the system is not having the encryption done or probably the patch is not correct. Probably it's the wrong version of an agent or it could be whatever it is. So all these sorts of things will start flagging as alleged to the SOC. Right, exactly. Or flag or a rebel flag. But if you come to, you know, like antivirus is not running properly or understanding with the older version or antivirus doesn't have the appropriate signature or the database or the database is not up to date.

We will monitor that. The health of the security tools is what we monitor there. And the production levels. So I think I need to go in depth to understand what the different parameters are. It's not just that it probably will come in and that's what the discussion is, right? Yeah, yeah, yeah. So, again, OK, let's look at this one. So that's what it says. You know, saw Sims or an idea. OK, so when you say this is you're nothing but your Yasim is the same solution which can be Splunk curate are outside involved. There are a lot of other solutions out there.

You know what it does. So in a nutshell, it's a huge database for storing the logs and a super agent sitting on top of it, sitting on top of the database and looking at each piece of the log and having its own algorithm up a lot. So if I think that OK, I've got a database, 250 GB of firewall logged. So that is a different one, logs and starts producing the reports. And that's what Brecon reports and dashboards. Right. Right. Which I love. Yeah. We'll go in depth as well. Yeah, I probably will. It's so. So is this what the engineering team actually does to set up these different parameters for these. So the engineering team is to set up the tools, configure the tools so they can use it. Right. Right. So I'm just showing you an example of a fortissimo, which is like out there for a demo.

OK, let's go to a dashboard. There's actually been plans to install Splunk onto my laptop at some point. You can do that. Spelunkers. For instance, you can definitely do that. There is a little quantitative data set data you can use, but yeah. So, you know, more or less like it looks like this, you know, you start their network interface stats for the device, your performance stats or even stats, your devices which are reporting like, you know, your network firewall parameter, your 40 demo, 40 web and you know, other devices which are reporting the data to this one can go into your system, DBI looks like. Yeah, you're your divisors, whatever is coming into this one, right?

What is logging in? So I guess it's more, more towards pulling the logs from different resources and trying to interpret them and trying to show them as an alert. Whenever there is something dramatic, an event happens. Right. And what it does is they go into the same console, they interpret the data and they write their own use cases as well. So sorry, let me take a step back. So what you are saying is that when you go to the CMB, there are many, many assets being configured in that, but two assets can have a similar kind of assets. Right. So what's the harm is it tries to compare them and then tries to give you a solution. That's telling. No, no. OK. So I probably will come back so that we just showed you. So, OK, so what happens is you're in a scene, you log multiple devices, right, so you lock your firewalls, your larger databases, your longer windows, authentication logs and everything else, all the infrastructure logs will come in, including your DNS, DTP, your if everything comes in.

And what happens is they'll come back into their own pockets. Right. It's more like imagining you're organizing an hour of 12th class or like seeing that in a school there are multiple classes. It's the same class one class two database, class three, email the fighting in their own sections so that you can clearly identify them and you attack them. And what your security does is it looks at that. It simply can't alert and report, which looks at the logs and says, OK, you know what, I think there is a pattern matcher based on activity from the logs. And it's like an alert like this one. You want your password usage for. What is this?

Non non guest network detected something like, you know, it just says it, then it says large outbound transfer identified. It sounds like it. OK, based on the amount of bytes sent out, it's time to write that. OK, you know what index is called the firewall, your source type of juniper. And it says, you know, the bytes out should be more than, say, to enter and be in ten minutes. Example. And you look at that incident, so you might I can probably show you what I understand from this is that you can correct me if I'm wrong, that this particular engine would already have a lot of predefined trend analysis answers to it for the problems that might arise typically.

But what happens to the ones which come as new issues or other new events which are not part of the pieces, and are only defined in the two? Yes. So for those, what happens is there are two ways to detect that. OK, one. You identify after an incident has been reported, you know what, there was some breach that happened, you were notified by a third party or by somebody else, you know something, get all these reports like that. Something is happening. I don't know what's happening. Right. So somebody else tells you you don't have any direction for that. So once you identify that and then you go back and start doing training for that, what are these?

You happen and then you try to find out what I think I should have a rule for. And it's more like reacting to a lawmaker reacting, right, just always is trying to react to instances and they get better at reacting at certain points to prevent or predict what can happen. Right? Yeah. So one is that the second thing is. Do you have a tool or detection tool in place, like in politics, in response tool, which puts them on the. Seeing that type of thing already, I don't know what is happening, but I feel it's suspicious. Why don't you go and look at it? So this is more like giving you a heads up stating that there might be a potential issue even coming your way to the street, to the scene. Something is happening.

I don't know what this is? OK, it's humoristic, you know, it's going to be a behavioral juristic thing. And this is from the end. Look at your server desktops point of view and mobile phones are exactly any. So anyway, something is wrong. I don't know what it is, but something is wrong. It's not a meeting department or audits. It's flagging some things. So let me flag it to you so that you could take it right. So that it can get into areas where it says, I failed to scan this file, but I like you. Right.

I found a file, which is I will send it to you right now, something like that. So that's the way you related devices. Because the thing is, you want to predict probably, you know, you can brainstorm and create use cases for that. But there will still be one new use case, a new alert or new attack methodology, which you'll never have understood. And I think it always, always is the reason why it's always exposed. Exactly. So the primary case of the primary case of the one that happened. Exactly.

So how do you think the attacker was able to come in? So which is the biggest company? It has got the top five hundred twenty that's got the US Army as our government. But how do you think the attack was? It was able to come in. The only thing was they were able to break into a user's password. And the way the SOC are, these guys are so identified by reviewing the authentication logs, they found a new user authentication from a different location or a set or a user logging in from a different location. That's how they identified that.

How would they know that the user is logging from a different mind? It could be restricted. You can log in from anywhere, right? Yeah, good question. So now you're working from home. You are in Malaysia. Imagine. On the original, expensive personal loss from Malaysia within 10 minutes, you also said some from tonight are from Bombay. What's the chances of some person traveling to India within 10 minutes from Malaysia? No, it's a generic idea or a little it's a VPN or something like that. Right.

But the question is, why would an expensive person be sorry, I'm taking names, but why would somebody log in from two different locations within a short span of time? It's an anomaly unless you're using a VPN, until they're using a vehicle. And the moment you see the IP address of the second login, you try to check again, you know, you put it in a bribe. You try to find out what this IP address is all about. And if you say that that is a malicious IP address or an act of reported earlier cases, immediately, that raises a flag saying that, you know, this access is malicious. That's what is called atypical travel or land speed alert, because you can't travel that fast, even by air or land to get to a different location. Right.

And that's that's a flag for you saying that why would somebody log in from two different places, even for example cases could be OK on an island, right? Yeah, on a log sent from, you know, machine number one. And he also locks in from machine number two, and suddenly I'm seeing authentications from four different machines from a different white. Why is it possible that one person is running from four different machines? Right. So that's a concern.

One one user login from multiple machines are one machine, one user trying to authenticate to four different machines. So I think I've seen this instance where they say that usually if the same user tries to log into three different systems and if it fails for more than three times, it becomes a major incident or something. Exactly. Exactly. So even if you do your Amazon Prime on Netflix, you try to log into it, flag a notification that you're not going to and say that you are the one who is doing it for them to understand that it's exactly the user who's doing this. And that's the multi factor authentication or Two-Factor. Yeah. So, OK, so again, coming back to SIM is nothing about your place where you record all the logs, your firewall logs or database logs and then try to call it.

Based on the event matches, right? Yeah, so you'll try to see that, OK, you know what has happened here? You will be able to use that behavioral policy detective mobile device from a system. Windows detection of possible rotten potatoes could be a site where they're trying to access or some kind of an access which is going on there. So when they say that they are trying to log into some website and then if it throws an incident, it means that when they try to access that website, it was probably trying to, you know, come back to this particular person who is trying to install some kind of or exactly.

There could be some maliciousness to the website or the website could already be tagged as malicious in our system. And that's how it's going to come down. All right. Already being a compromise. It's a compromise. Yeah. Yeah, exactly. So that's where the second piece comes in. The simple solution is you understand the situation and probably give you a better example of that as your Alienware solution. But again, you know, so that's one it's basically a legalistic workspace with your security engineer there.

You write your rules and there you have your alerts to get in. There you have your reports in there based on your compliance requirements, based on your SOC requirements. What do you want , like what are they trying to monitor right now? Yeah. The alien world. Yes. Yeah. OK, just just to be sure. So that's what SIM does. So SIM is your core of your alerting mechanism in an environment because you can integrate all the solutions in there and then go and brainstorm, look at the log, write a rule and then have it flagged and then create a recipe for that, create a process for that creative incident task checklist for that when something good happens.

What do you do? Right. So that's our primary solution for and it's like a log log aggregation and then alerting mechanism for you. Then comes your server, which is your security orchestration and automation response. Right. So what would he be able to share with me so that I would have a better understanding at some point of time just in case if I have to tell them I should be doing the interview? Yep, I would be. I get to create some things and send it across to you. Be great. Yeah. So let's do this. Do. Security. Hmm. So it could be, you know, to them big, that's too. One little. OK.

I'll show you a cheat sheet for. Mark. Oh, there you go. One. OK, so this could be more like an issue before you will be more formal. It's an operator. It has got a lot of steam to charge everything in that just for a newbie to understand. But in a nutshell, this is what you do. It's a single page cheat sheet or a checklist for handling an incident. Right. So there are two things you do when you handle an incident. There is one, a redacted checklist like, you know, if you know if you've done some flying or if you've seen some flying videos, what does a pilot do when they see them before they fly the plane? They have a checklist in place. OK, flaps, redacted or, you know, gear down or whatever that is, or engines on agents in the 30 percent or blah, blah, blah, that they go to the checklist and they agree that this is what am I supposed to do before taking flying a pilot, by the way, am I you know that, right? Exactly.

You know that, right? That's exactly what's happening. So you might put yourself in the same perspective and you are running. You have to have a checklist, right? What am I going to do when an incident happens? This is what I'm going to use, an automated sandbox. What does behavioral analysis do?

What is a control tool? What to do? What am I going to look for? What am I going to get the malware analysis tool reversing to this one of the other vendors, other vendors? It's a fight, I think CIA based, which was released after the hack happened. For which is the following? No, no, no, before that, there was a hack on Friday or before that I think there was. Right. OK, yeah. Yeah. So. I'm just going to look at it. Other things. Oh. So an example could be a critical log-in checklist example, right? So what you do is, you know, a critical logorrhea checklist. So generally I defy the sources and automated tools that you can use during the analysis, copy the logs, record a single location where you are able to review them.

Your simulation, right? Yes, potentially security sources, server and workstation, your application logs, your security tools all by proxy. So I'll share this link with you. This is a beautiful link. You should definitely spend some time never going to that. So this is what you do from a logging point of view, like what do you log on what you monitor? So typical log locations, your always windows, what to look for and what to look for. And windows from a very unique perspective right now for network devices, other resources. What do you look for on Web servers? Right. So these are some of the use cases which you and I will talk about in the future from an attack perspective.

So this is something that you have to look for. So based on this, your whole incident response office will be created. Right. So analyzing normalizes malicious documents. So what you do is you write a piece of paper analyzing a malicious document to some of your sources that I have a go to phishing email. Why don't you analyze it? OK, what am I going to use for a general approach for document analysis, examine the document, look at them. But it could extract suspicious code, identify the relevant officers, obfuscate code, disassemble the code and understand the next steps of infection.

In a nutshell, these are the six steps of our SUV which can span 10 pages, right? Yeah, exactly. So because now it's your take, listen to what I am going to do from when I'm flying something that I'm actually in the incident. When you're in a simulator flying an airplane, the whole experience is different. But, you know, this is you don't want to run through ten different pages of what you do on step eight, but you have one page where you're telling me what exactly to do. So you have your recipes, you have your checklist or your cheat sheet, whatever.

This looks very, very close to more or less like a checklist, but a compass version of it. Exactly. So this is exactly what we are trying to do here in our mission is like, you know, have recipes for formal audit requirements where a new guy comes in, he goes through the whole procedure of what's happening. But after you get experience, you don't want to refer to this piece. You want to refer to something as a teacher checklist. Yeah, right. On a high level. At a high level. So when you're handling it, you just have it on a piece of paper.

You print it out or you have it on another screen. You look at it and you start doing it. Yeah. So you have your recipes and you have your checklist. That's how you try to have a documentation perspective. Right. Is the same for all the socks. Are they exclusive? Um, you can call it the playbook, you can call it the checklist. So what happens. But with some of our agencies you have a playbook which is again used for your search solutions. So your new book example could be your SO. Nable. It could be this playbook.

So it's a floor diagrammatically floor diagram which says that's what you need to do from a Decision-Making perspective. Right. And usually these playbooks will go into a tool which looks at this and then makes the decision for you or do the steps for you. So if you're saying that, OK, you OK, so you have a solution, which we are just about to talk about now, which is an artificial solution. OK, Splunk, or your simple solution to the alert is out there and your source solution receives it and now it implements a playbook, which is this one here. So let's suppose Splunk receives a notification from a user saying that he reported a phishing email for another tool which sounded like he's using Outlook and they're using Coffin's fishmeal.

What are the other tools, the report, if it comes to your solution and your user has a playbook to handle a phishing incident. Right. So the email is this year. It passes the email for evaluation. OK, what it does, it looks at two things. One, it looks at a user, an attachment. So you're telling you're creating the flow of what you do and putting that on the Florida floor. Right. Right. So it's like driving a car or driving a plane or something, you stop, you said, OK, I'll go through the checklist. And that's what your evaluation checklist is.

You know, you have your Parramatta checklist, everything is done, all your hydraulics, everything is done. Now you start the engine, you get the permission for everything is clear, you know, the flight plan and you just go, boom. Right. And that's what it does. So once he makes a decision, he does the floor diagram. OK, if after the first is aborted, what do I do? If the flight is going smoothly, what is the next waypoint I'm going to go? That's what it does. This is an automated image. It's on autopilot.

Everything is done from the autopilot. Part of it does everything for you, but at certain times of the situation, you'll tell your autopilot that you stop and get me. I have to intervene before you make a decision there. Yeah, the manual kicks in. Right. That's what happens. The solution is security orchestration to orchestrate and automate some responses, but not everything. So this story is basically the orchestration to understand that. But so what it does is it would automatically go and fix the problem by following some checklist that is exactly, exactly right. So what example in this case?

What happens is, you know, if there is a quarrel, there's an attachment here. The content of attachment completely has to Aristotle, which is on the side where you take the ashes if it is malicious. I know it automatically sends a correction or a request to or maybe a request to the backend system for getting it right, right. Imagine you put the same condition that if the email is from a CEO or a seasoned employee or a C suite in the highest leadership level, raise a flag to talk and talk, will make a decision for you.

So the tool is not making automatic decisions, but the sarcastic interpretation and saying that you don't want to delete an email for us is sweet, but you want to understand and pull your CEO and have him tell us what exactly needs to be done next. So sorry is basically a combination of all the soapies into one single junk, except by somebody writes a solution on the back end by using a code of APIs, let's say, or plug ins, and then this would just go and interact with all the other planes which are attached to it in action on them. Right? Exactly. Exactly. So what happens is if you see here, a security incident comes, the alert to your flaws, the workflow begins and there is a response.

So for every one in the playbook, there's an automated task. If you see this, do this. So if the response is either it's in a document or it's automated, you know, if the IP is malicious, Richard, the firewall demonizes to block it or directly go block it in the firewall or block the e-mail address or the sender or receiver or something like that, or send a notification to talk to you for the next chapter and then does the next chapter, what send out a notification to the user that your email has been blocked. So imagine.

If you take the sword out of the picture, it's EMU's, which is doing this manual process. So what you do is with a sword, you remove the manual process and have the tool do the steps for you. So basically, if I did not have, I would have to hire more engineers to go into it, everything my mentor is doing is automated. That's the difference, but also it's kind of like maintaining a knowledge management database where people have all the prerequisites. What are the scenarios being done? But if they do not have those scenarios as part of the or that is, then how would they approach, for example, some kind of incident comes into place and then you would probably see or detect that I may even club and then it wants to go and fix it.

But then if the store does not have a solution for it or it can fix it, then would it stop or would it through again some kind of an alert? Yeah. So the question is if. OK, so there is an alert. What do you mean I'm sorry. You know, it's just an event management incident, and event management or simply the CFO seems so. Yes, some solution triggers an alert. If you don't have overflow, your sword will not be able to do anything. Yeah, you can have something that if you see this is not the reason for that. To that, you know, you have a new alert which is received. So at the time, what happens is, you know, there are bigger organizations. There are two things.

One is the engineering team, which is a contract writing team which manages the team solution as well as the content and manages this as well. So when they have a news alert in a solution or a new report, they'll automatically go and create the process in association. That's how the process should be, because they can't, they can't put on alert and never create a floor diagram or respond diagram in the source solution. Right. Yeah, yeah, sure, I mean, if there is something not able to detect it, obviously they need to come up with a new floor, which is exactly how they should be having. So that's how the engineering team really works. But even a small container, 15 demoralization.

The stock itself is a team. Differences between who doesn't and doesn't need any work. The manager uses cases, they use cases. They'll maintain the use cases as well. Today they happen. That's what my team does. I have a small team of Levington members where we do everything we like, the way that they use cases we find in these cases, we have this opportunity. You have the response plans that we have the checklist ready. There's a whole process for that. But in a different orientation, talk is a different response to the content management team.

Yeah, yeah, I believe that's the reason why this particular Petronius, you know how big it is. Right. So obviously they want to have a separate engineering team and they also asked me to come up with some kind of a project management methodology whereby these things can run different projects. But anyways, that's going to be a part of the other job description, too, because that is more towards it. So I think we're going to talk about it later, whatever time it is. Yep, yep, yep. So, yep. So if you see this, you know that this is exactly the floor diagram.

I don't know. Can you see that? But it's just that it's not that. Yeah. I just did it. We can just jump to the browser and then. You see this? Yeah, so this is exactly the floor diagram that would look like a solar solution, right? OK, execute the block indicators that there is a playbook for that so you can write playbooks inside the playbook, right to play because nothing but your whatever investigations, if you have defined in the document, you put it as a floor and to follow this process and the tool for that for you. And that's where the story is all about.

So they'll remove this redundant manual task out of the picture. So if you have an example, how do you better utilize human talent is what the bigger question is. So if you have a 10 minute team member team and you're having close to four hundred and twenty alerts every day in 24 hours, so you have two hundred alerts per day, but shift close to two hundred dollars per shift. So yeah, imagine and there are major incidents. What happens to the other incidents? Can you then you're able to focus on the other hundreds of interests as not everything. Right. So then if people are out sick, what am I going to do?

If there is a little person with media, what are you going to do in this case? The sod will come into the picture. What it does is for the low and medium severity. It automates the all action center to the user. Does the action on behalf of the user. So that analyst so that I don't need to go and do the manual job. Yeah, right. So all the logic, whatever I do, is already built into the playbook, no matter how complex the playbook is right to build this thing. And that's how the tool basically reacts and does the activity. So when the stock receives alerts, these all come in the form of logs, but not all the events will be coming to only a few become incidents. Yes. Yes.

So what is the threshold for them to become incidents? Is there a specific criteria? It's a. We just show you something, probably that's. Uh, I had a good diagram for the Spanker funnel. It was a beautiful picture, which represents exactly the question which you ask right now. OK, let me find out later then maybe I'll have a little reminder. Logs to Alert's. So I just need to know what the criteria are and how, yeah, the criteria, the criteria differ, right? So, yes, for every act you can't have the same threshold. For example, for example, in this case, let's see this.

You know, you have this one. You have your customer facing data. You have your outside the data center, you have your network databases, applications cloud your little windows. Right. So you have all these data sources, for Windows and Linux, you might have some Gibby's of data coming. Your firewalls will have almost 50 or 60 GB of data, which is coming in every day.

Liquidity data coming from your Windows and Linux. Right. So what do I do here? So there is so much data coming in. You write a rule on that. So what does that rule basically say that, OK, I have a rule in place, for example, could be a password being attacked on my Windows authentication lot. Right. So I'm saying that, OK, on the authentication logs, I'm going to see that passwords being attacked would basically mean that attackers would spring it, just spray the password on multiple users.

So what they do is they use a single password and they use the closing accounts, read the same password with the same user, multiple user accounts and see what breaks. Right. At least some ways one could match somebody. One could match, but it could be a brute force. You know, it could be Windows, brute force attack where you're trying to brute force an account with multiple passwords, right? Yeah, that could happen. So there the threshold is there that the threshold for you could be saying that.

Login failures from 10 different users in five minutes, then they then it's going to be a huge incident or something like, yeah. The threshold is very minimal because the threshold also matches the time duration as well. The threshold, not just the amount of activity which you're seeing, but how long have you seen this? So you see in 30 seconds resolve like right now, if you see one hundred and five hundred A, B or one G be transferred into 10 minutes from a firewall. Right.

If multiple users are going to benefit the resolution later. I think that, you know, multiple single user logging and four for four different machines, it's a five minute resolution. So the threshold is four machines in five minutes. That's why the threshold is. And for that you'll have a security criticality or criticality is there. And then, you know, your response times are there and that's how you define your response times. Yeah, right. So that's how you understand the thresholds. So let me copy the address and then give it to you so that you get along with the logs. Or maybe if you can give me a few links.

What do I phase out from the especially as you're putting in the chart? I will be great. Would you mind if I just take a break? Absolutely. I was about to ask you, you want to break or you know I don't. I just want to go too quickly. Please go. Yeah, yeah, yeah. I just need to get a quick coffee. So cyclodextrin, you understand the simple solution. What do you do? So this is exactly what I wanted to show. So you will log close to a billion logged days and just say every day, then you will. So it's not when you say you invest blank, you mean you don't log everything. So imagine you you're getting some did you like your it's like moving boxes of data radio or shifting a house saying that, you know, when you are moving the boxes, so what you do the moment you move the boxes, you'll put them in up in initial storage area and screen them, you'll rip the wrapper off and then throw the boxes off you around the to store the boxes. That's right.

But you'll discard the unnecessary items there. And then only the locks which are necessary inside your processing area, which is your profiler indexing area. So after you filter your index and you start analyzing the events, then you'll call it when I see the correlation is nothing but within the Luxor's or between two different sources. Right. So imagine you saying that, OK, an authentication attempt came for a particular user and it failed. Right, but if I have a technology platform logging into Splunk or any other platform there and it flags the I lost the rule, say that, OK, you're not going to go into the index for threat intelligence as well as verify the IP address.

Come back and, you know, give me the status of it, whether it's malicious or not, and then we'll make our next decision. Right. So that's how the coalition is coordinating multiple events or multiple data sets of logs and trying to make a judgment call. OK. Right. Either it can be saying that, OK, now you got an alert from an IP address which was seen for its application, but one of them, one Web application. So you'll also want to check whether this IP was also doing the same activity for other Web applications. Then you left the right coalition for those indexes or those logs. That's right. And then you see that. OK, I want to check whether I was able to get into this application.

I also need to check and verify whether it was seen in other indexes for ideology types like windows and authentication, whatever that is. And then you try to correlate that different data set and say, OK, what I saw that I did not see, if you saw it, you'll reason alone did not see it. You'll probably have a different degree of alarm. Right. So that's how correlation needs your correlating multiple. Right, and then what you do is once the threshold is so even if you're logging a log or I don't know how many of our logs, your logging, not everything will turn out to be an accident.

Only the rules which have been created or the alert will just be built in. Will when the collision matches the threshold matches, then it'll come back and, you know, kind of like an alarm. It can be something which you have written as an alert or something. A vendor itself has written an alarm or the alert, except the log itself is flagged as a malicious activity, right? Yeah. So that's how you kind of are. So, I guess when we say that it's a lot of interest, this basically all the logs, the entire let's say we have about on the DVD that we did, which probably one is what probably is our interest area right now, who does that 99 percent scrubbing from the hundred percent? Is that the tool?

It's automatically being done by the developers who develop this tool. Yeah. The simple solution will give you a suggestion of what to log on, what not to log. And so there is something called your logging specifications. So let me show you as well that. So this is called the long cheat sheet. OK, so what is the log, for example, for Windows in Splunk, what do you need to log? What are the activities you should log ? This is an example of it, right? So it is a critical event to monitor in Windows logs. So a new start, new process, starting user log on shared access or shiitakes. She had access to a new service, installed interconnections, file auditing registry, auditing expenses, expenses, expenses. Right.

So let me just give you this link so that you have a great time. Yeah, so now there's this logging, we'll tell you what to log, what type of event log from the windows itself. So when you're adding a Windows event, windows, even logging, or when you're pulling all the windows, even while Windows servers in Splunk and then you have one config file. So what happens is every system will have a conflict file. Which is more to say, every expert will have a conflict, yet every asset type will have a conflict file in your solution. OK, so where's my network? So every asset type will have our log source will have an index file or a conflict file where you say what you're supposed to log. Right.

And you know what you're supposed to think so they can be two things. One, you can configure the log or configure or edit the configuration on the simple solution to pull the required logs and drop certain logs. And, ah, you can also set the logging at the source of where the log is getting the latest example, your firewall. So if you vote with firewalls, you'll say, you know the logging level, right. It's warning info. What about logging level your Saturday, right. If you say that you need to log everything informational and you should like everything.

So it means you'll get alerts in your Splunk solution, then in Splunk, what you visit. OK, do you send me everything for me? I am more interested only in worrying about, so I will set the config file to only track and just the data which is an and drop everything else which is not required. Right. So I understand. Let me reiterate what I understood. Basically in the Splunk, just taking this as a base example for Sam, right? So what we're saying is that every other type will definitely have some kind of a configuration file, probably an indexing file.

And then based on which, you know, their specifications would be set across what should be logged and what not should be logged in the same solution. Yes. It's not like though you're getting everything doesn't mean that you have to log everything into your solution. Right. You're going to begin to see it again. You know, again, this whole thing comes back to probably another topic. You just called your audit login specifications and your logging logs standards in your own organization. What is your organization interested in logging?

Yeah, so when you're and that dictates what comes into your team as well. Right, right. So if you're saying that my relatives should be or should have anything beyond reasonable, should come into some solution, that's how you say that, because the standard is that, you know, your login specification for a doctor or a switch is information about you. So first your leader said it said the login specifications in your log levels in your firewall where the auditing is enabled.

And then and then put the same logs into Splunk and configure your day log indication in your Splunk or solve simple solutions that you know what you have to specifically choose and bring it in tomorrow. It should not be that suddenly there is some configuration change on the source or on the firewall. And you are also getting information and suddenly you're logging from 66 percent to 20 people that you know should not be. So you should have checks in both the places that you know, you have along there in the firewall level. You are seeing this simple solution.

Make sure that you are looking for the warning tag and then login only those things and discard everything else. So all this data would be discarded, all of which only one debate would remain based on what you ask people and not exactly hundreds of examples could be just one example. Yeah. So if you're seeing hundreds of people in one solution, yes. But hundreds overall would still be at the end of discarding everything. Yeah, exactly. That's what I mean. So that is what we would look at. Yeah.

I probably will start analyzing that data, which is what in terms of your requirements that you have set across the parameters that he said across means I need to have anything which is about one thing or probably which is the transit or whatever. It could be the status at the point of time for your given asset or asset type, right? That's what happened. So then the other other kind of perspective you need to do this one is why do you so how long do you want to store it? Right. Because other than compliances then you need to have a detention policy and that's it.

You use a simple solution because you get the retention policy of what your company has. A dictator, either it is hot and it is cold, which gives you an extra day off, but it isn't so they can go and carry a log if there is an incident which you want to previously record and try to understand. So, you know, you retain the logs for further or historic correlation as well. Yeah, right. So that allows you to store that 60 DB and say, OK, I call it, I can carry the logs historically and try to find out what has happened. But yeah, just out of curiosity, what is the baseline for the ordinary comment to keep the number of logs? I mean, how long was that before?

If you're in a financial condition, if you're dealing with a financial organism, they will set a standard saying that, you know, what do you have one hundred and eighty days or do you have a 90 day retention period? Whatever is your company standard is that it all depends upon the compliance. The idea says I saw audited compliance regulations which are falling as well. I don't think the government at length wants you to retain for a longer duration like how your trade but predicted your, you know, your telecom providers to have a seven year old or something like that.

You know, don't you don't want to do it because it's a cost for the company, but compliance bit them to have longer periods. So, again, you know, so from a high level understanding perspective, this is you know, it's like your sim your when you say your tip is nothing but your threat intelligence platform. It is nothing but your threat intelligence. Oh, that is that threat intelligence, but that's OK. Yeah. So you have a lot of platforms out there. You have your audience, which is an open source platform. You have MSP, which is your manager. I forgot about that, but am I there? Then you have your pictures, personal video, recorded feature or your autofocus autofocus, which is also a great resource that a lot of others also like is there for the government organizations, which provides you threat intelligence. Right.

And so basically that is nothing but your IP bad. You are doing bad domains. Bad activity type is bad, some sensitive information is bad. So they provided this intelligence, which allows you to enhance your detection platform and enhance the data that you're gathering that enhances your detection ability. So your example is when you get a firewall alert, you make notes. I probably have. And I'm just a. So, yeah, I'll probably type it here, your tip is finding what is but it gave me a lot of tips, you know, on the platform, which is nothing but your or the X from Alien World or. Cawdor Shiho. Or it can be I think it can be your or your homeland. Briefs. So your homeland, your CIA or homeland briefs or the U.S., FBI, those can be on all intelligence sources, so.

So there is a tool which my organization uses called a. Well, while many people came to this tool, what it does is it also threatens but it's more towards. What's happening with your organization, so what it does is if you see the screen there, if you see the screen here, you have multiple tabs here, right? Oh, I'm sorry. I'm sorry. Yeah, OK. So this is nothing but your security from your perimeter like perimeter. When you see that's what it does, you give this tool your domain and Euripides. And that's pretty much it. So what it does is in a Web notification, it says that, you know, maybe mid-band dot com invite. So there was something which I found for that domain.

There is a subdomain for that same primary domain, which is the iPhone. And there is an app. There is a malicious application or malicious code posted on that. Right. Or people who are adequately used to build a website example. OK, so then what you do is you go and look at the website and say that, OK, you know what, there is a third party that could be using it as malicious. I want to make sure that, you know, my application is protected from that attack or should not be using this malicious script to kind of breach my website. Right. Then you have your incidents or code repositories where there was accord with your company's name on that, which is GitHub or any other code repositories. Right.

So it identifies that it constantly scans your GitHub or leader code repositories on Interex. Do you know what? There are some things that your company's name you might want to take a look at. Right. So why would we use that tape when we already have a solution in place, a monitoring solution in place? Good question. So what it does is so this is a third party. This is an excellent company which is not looking at what is happening inside your organization. OK, so this is a completely independent body, independent of adulate monitors, your organization from the outset of it.

It doesn't look from the inside, but it looks from the outside. So it could be the type of squatting domain which is like, you know, maybe dot com that my embassy is a site. Right. So what it does is it might let me give you an example. So it says. I've been doing the check. Yeah, just yeah, yeah, you see that I did the reason I did it. Yeah, correct. Correct. Or it could be me, baby. I also saw that I just got out of coincidence this morning. Somebody was saying, Maybank dot com. You see the difference.

One of the letters would be a different one, for example, which is actually the area it could be coming from. So what happens is these are all types of squatting or cybersquatting. Right. And this is also what sort of monitors? So cybersquatting, cybersquatting, is it a type of squatting or because there are various. I don't mean to. Boom. It's called the. So let's go back home. So you know what it does now, it does all the variants of the same Maybank God come by and tell you how many domains are available. You see? Oh, OK, and what it does is this is only giving you 250, but actually it gives you 10000 different variations of that. Right.

And what it does is it looks at all the variance of it and then takes how many of them. It doesn't even it doesn't just check the domains, the type of spending, but it doesn't take hold generally. And that makes us a case saying that, OK, are you not talking to the legal team and legal team will go and tell the domain, the ISP saying that if you don't do it, we'll have a case against you and then, you know, please take it on because it's actually intimidating or imposing, like my organization. Right. Yes. So that's another use case, why wait, wait, my organization uses imagery, but also what it does is the best thing, which I find is it looks at dark and deep web and looks at all the databases there.

If there is a breach database which is exposed, which is dumped there it goes and looks at. The dot com, like, you know, example, if I'm in a company called me bank dot com that invites if there is an e-mail, I recall, you know, Kumar addressed labor and got a dot com that anybody it look for that email addresses with that domain and could find anything it stereotactic that, you know, I saw one of your company's references in one of the breaches there. So it will also look at all the documents, it means that the ones which are actually being prosecuted are under the federal investigation are probably malicious websites or could be anything, as a matter of fact.

So this would also search all of it externally. But because it's the same tool cannot be configured to the external Internet for some reason, this third party would go into it. So what we don't want to expose are some cities for abuse, only support for internal use. But this tool is holstered on the Internet and this guy is trying to do the attacks on behalf of us. If I do the testing on behalf of me, I am exposing my my ISP or my IP changes to the external vendor or to the to the to the attackers because the attacker can sit anywhere the attacker can anywhere in the country that you want to use this type of tools which is doing on behalf of you and not telling others that these things, you know, for some company.

It's not like, I think Alaska, right? Yeah, you know, it doesn't discount the Internet for the present and tells you if it finds any hits for you. Right. OK, so, Brian. So, again, that's what I'm doing and I'm doing a dark web exclusive test for, you know, for this domain name and dot com, if there are any hits, it'll tell me that, you know, there were some mentions about some business there. So that's one example I can give you. So it's powerful. It does help to cover a lot of areas where they are. They will struggle to do that or they'll have to set up their own tests for that.

All right, so it could be your security. It can be mobile apps or it can be any of the platforms which are there, which is a discovery for that. So it does you know, external attacks are very security compliance incidents, non-intrusive technology, instant notification, if you get notifications straightaway to the mailbox of what you're getting. Right. So it could be a network saying that there's a new IP which is found in your organization, which is hosting a domain state.

It could be a mobile application which is found or it could be your Web application. We just found them. I don't know why this guy just gave one, which would have given the incident response there, but. Yeah. So any questions so far? I'll probably have to stop here and ask you for any questions. If you have any, I'm good to go. OK, good. So that's all yours or sip and dip. So the entire area is nothing but. A super beefed up version of your orienteers. Is it much more than what your endurance does traditionally? Yep, once again. Yeah. Yeah, so it does much more than your anti-war resolution. End point, detection and response.

Responsible king and queen. So this is one, if you can see my screen. Let me call here. Can you see? Yeah, yeah, so this is an idiota Cul-De-Sac is an idiot. OK, so there are two to two things here. One is either the other one is XDR. I'll talk about experience. I talk about it here in one direction. The response to this is much beyond your traditional endurance. So what does it do? It has a and a middle built into that artificial intelligence and machine learning that a lot of heuristic behavioral based what can attack a do working attacker go what he can do, jump from what tools he will use.

And everything is built into this one. It's like a human behavioral thinking that comes almost exactly like, you know, when you have a hammer. That's what it does. And look at your operating system behavior. What does it do, you know, and then try to detect some activity. The thing is, ETR is built on a framework which is called Meital. Is built on microtechnology technology because it's a framework, it's a framework. So when you look at this one, this is exactly what your framework is. So you have your OK. So what does attack mean?

It's trying to help understand a soccer team, these steps, how an attacker will try to plan. So what it does is the attacker will try to provoke a reconnaissance question. He'll scout his target first. Then once you understand the loopholes, then he'll try to do resource development. Right. You'll try to compromise the infrastructure, compromised the account. Then once he has done the initial initial attempt, then he'll do the initial access of trying to compromise some things. Right now, he can develop capabilities to perform the attack, then once he is against the initial axis, he does the execution.

After the execution is done, he'll maintain persistence. That means he'll try to gain a foothold in the organization. I like to share this link with you here. Yeah. Then what happens is then he'll approve legislation. So example could be he performs he compromises a level one analyst or level one accountant or level one organization or person would have just had a really excellent but. Exactly, exactly. And then he'll raise his escalated privileges from that level to the highest admin level. Yeah, right. Then what he does is he does evasion.

How can he evade detection? You know, what are some of the inbreed tools in the Windows operating system that you can use to defend or evade detection? Right. Then how he access credentials, then how he will perform. Discovered the inauguration after he's in the organization. Then how can he move laterally from one system to the other without getting detected? Then how can he collect the information right then? How can he perform command and control where he can establish a base from there he can start doing some more damage to the region from there.

How can an external trade data outside of the organization and then trade, then it's the impact of what he can do. What's the impact of. And he does all these things and that's what my dad tells you, is the attack framework of how attackers come and do that and then what, as a blue team or something. But what we do is we look at, OK, you know what, in reconnaissance, what he can do, he can gather victim's identity information from multiple sources.

He can gather victims into organizing information from multiple sources. He can look at, you know, search for open websites that use Jordan to access website information or simply like, you know. Yeah, so this is, again, I'm just saying, you know, a reconnaissance example, so you have what you're going to use it for. So your name and dot com. If the website is built on Akamai DNS, it has email hosting SBF, Central policy framework is enabled. We have SSL certificates, we have global certificates. Right.

And these are the technologies, which is what it is, which is using which it is using. The site is using the bulletin. Now, let's look at Google GOOG. I've got a new keyboarder, the. So you see, it says you said it has got a framework which has got to be content delivery, JavaScript advertising operating system. If I can, I can fingerprint so many things here. I can see so many things here, so this is what an attacker would do from understanding how big it is from a Web application perspective, what it's there.

So he would find a gap there or try to find a vulnerability so that he can enter in the tools or in the tools, which is which the application is built with. If there is a problem there, he'll try to exploit that. Right. And that's what your, you know, reconnaissance is. And then we will, as a blue team, go through each one of them and try to anticipate how I can detect some stuff when it happens here. Right.

But will there be any scenarios for me for this kind of situation, for the FBI, or is it better to come up with all of these solutions? I like orchestras. Exactly. So the attack involves. This has become the industry standard for every tool to match up for you. Yeah.So these are your ETR tools. I'll share this link with you as well. So what happens is this Meitav framework is so strong and it has made so much presence in the last two or three years, four years is what all the vendors are trying to do. See that my tool detects maximum MicroTech attacks or MicroTech scenarios, whatever you are. It's depicted here. Right, and they try to do what the media does. It gives them a body, which is a pretty group, advanced persistent threat group, like a Chinese group or Russian group or a Ukrainian group or a youth group or what are the groups?

And they'll give them a group. And has the agency stolen the system and run this attack? And she also advanced a persistent threat. OK, yeah, APD, OK, so an example could be, let's say Kotick. So what you do is in the crowd say you go back and look at LPT 29 or or carbamazepine seven, which is a financial Russian, you know, we call it a gummy bear. Gummy bear, not the gummy bear, but a grizzly bear. Yeah, exactly. So, uh, Russian cyber bear and actually the grizzly bear. Sorry, it's a fancy bear. So a fancy name was given to the Russian attackers. Right. OK, so what happens here is.

OK, so this attack was running on an agent on a system where a Kozik agent with an idiot agent was installed. Right. OK, so what do you do if you go back here, look at executions, OK? What did they do? So it did detect an attack where it's saying that there was. There was some Winward execution there, right? Let's look at what the attack was. So the attack was a tactical configuration, change of direction, a tactic, a tactic named Miko's malicious macro execution was generated when we launched it. And this is how the aerial platform detected it. This is how it was what the beauty of the ideal solution is. It would represent the attack in a pictorial form, like how the attack started from where it started, like Vinewood started it. It's part of the script. It's in another script.

Then it's on to the commander Dixy, apart from Commander Dexedrine, another script, and then starts going on doing some activity there. Right. So it shows you the process, the execution map, and tells you exactly what to do, other than what it does? It automatically blocks the execution of that. OK, right, it blocked the execution of that and then. Allows the responder, which is Sakti, to network in the system, if you see the option the network can deal with, allow me to simply just click it and the machine is off the network. OK, it allows for an instant solution to avoid the threat, correct?

Exactly. But imagine your traditional tourist never had this capability to detect Doderer Block, but it will not block any serious attacks and can actually do the action. You know, I have to go manually counting the machine, but the idea has the framework in place. It understands the different types of attacks. It has a signature for malicious attacks as well as the signature based attacks, as well as the might of the attacks where they anticipate and look at those scenarios, Brock's execution and saying that, you know, I'll block the execution. But if you want to do it, you can control the machine as well. OK, right.

But what scenarios would we use the idea? All the places' biggest scenario is covid work from home. So let's talk about that. So you are running a sock or you are running a company. You suddenly have to work from home, you are worried about what your employees do using the official laptop without the VPN. The possibilities are endless, they can go to Netflix, they can go to Amazon Prime, they can go to any—site, they can do anything for that matter. Right. They give it to the kids because they could do it so that they can install anything on that. So how do you protect that?

And still allow the ability to control that machine. Well, there needs to be a remote agent being installed. Yeah. So instead of doing that, you can solve your solution. So it provides you the protection, allows the talk to monitor the machine and contain the machine and investigate the machine, even if it's connected to VPN or not VPN. But it still needs to have an agent installed on the left, obviously. Yeah, it does. To have an agent on that right. Instead of having multiple agencies on that.

You know, this one agent does almost everything for you. Yeah. OK, so I get your point so you don't need to have a simulation or whatever it is. But if you have any area in place and it's going to help you, you need a simple solution. The system is different. The SIM is the log aggregator. It collects what the tool is doing, you know. So imagine, you idiot. Do you still need antivirus logs to go into some solution? So Sara is not a protection mechanism. It's only a log aggregator which allows me to ingest the logs and have rules we can understand or monitor activity. But an immediate solution is on.

The endpoint is protecting in real time, blocking something in realtime from happening. OK. Justin. And actually, can I say that so it's protecting and actually, yes, on the easier it is detection in response to they will tell you that you're detecting and responding to it immediately. So that's what the beauty of it here is. It can do a lot. It can show you a lot of my company's solutions. But unfortunately, I can't show the console because I left my job, then I heard. Does this mean that the EPA has to be installed on all the assets or is it only for the endpoints, servers, desktops, wherever you think you need to? But yeah, firewalls will not be able to have Edir because that's not an operating system. As per say, the execution doesn't happen or the processing doesn't happen. OK, so basically there's only one endpoint. Yes. Endpoint your mobile's Linux Windows laptop, desktop, Max, correct. Yeah, yeah, yeah. The name itself is easier. So no, the more questions you ask the more clarity you'll get.

Don't worry about asking questions. Okay. So it does give you this pictorial way of doing it. And it kind of is something called as. So the area is more prominently known for something called living off the land tax. No living off the land or living off the land. So when I'm saying living off the land, imagine you going into a forest. And what do you do, you don't have anything to eat. So you live off the land, right?

You find food, whatever the forest is providing CMB, the attacker also does the same thing when he's in the bin, when it's in the organization that he lives off the land, which uses windows capabilities against itself. Right, actually, an example is making the operating system vulnerable by itself. Yeah, he uses such an example. I'll ask you, because of how many ways can you access a website? Oh, well, by knowing the domain name or the IP, which I mean, what would you use to access the main or accessible website? Browser, anything else?

Links emailing the authorities in different ways that we can come across. What if I say, you know, we can use a notepad to do that? Well, I did not know that. So let's do that. See what is happening here. You dumped the entire website in the notepad. We don't get it right, so now imagine the attack. So now imagine the attacker does this and runs a command center to open a notepad, opening the door. Come on, run the website, dump it, dump it in a file. But I then imagine he's going to be upset that what he's downloading is not the content, so he'll download a script using Notepad and save it in a different location and then go make a copy of that notepad, convert and rename the two ideas and run the script.

So he will never use any browser for that. And so he basically used a notepad to go out. So he's living off the land. Right would just go and compile that code and then he can do anything and he can do anything. Exactly. And that's what it says living off the land. He doesn't use the additional tools, but he used tools within the organization. It could be a network.

Conclusion

Conclusion. This brings us to the end of this Book. You now hopefully have enriched your understanding of the political system. I am very glad to have shared my knowledge with you.

I hope that you find it just as invaluable as I did. I really hope you have enjoyed this Book. I have certainly enjoyed teaching you. If you want to learn more about the way we operate as part of a group and how our society influences us, check out my Book on sociology. Goodbye.

Don't miss out!

Visit the website below and you can sign up to receive emails whenever SADANAND PUJARI publishes a new book. There's no charge and no obligation.

https://books2read.com/r/B-A-YJFBB-RMLRC

BOOKS 2 READ

Connecting independent readers to independent writers.

Also by SADANAND PUJARI

Master The Psychology Of Weight Loss Via Hypnosis Build
Healthy Sleep Habits Learn The Art Of Meditation
Improve People Management And Build Employee
Engagement
Content Marketing Masterclass Create Content That Sells
Cyber Security For Normal People Protect Yourself Online